NEXT GENERATION LEADERSHIP

NEXT GENERATION LEADERSHIP

How to Ensure Young Talent
Will Thrive with Your Organization

ADAM KINGL

HarperCollins
LEADERSHIP

An Imprint of HarperCollins

Published by HarperCollins Leadership,
an imprint of HarperCollins Focus LLC.

Book design by Aubrey Khan, Neuwirth & Associates.

ISBN 978-1-4002-1561-4 (eBook)
ISBN 978-1-4002-1547-8 (HC)

Library of Congress Control Number: 2019953545

Printed in the United States of America
20 21 22 23 LSC 10 9 8 7 6 5 4 3 2 1

CONTENTS

FOREWORD

In the last year, I've had the opportunity to facilitate a number of strategic planning sessions for companies in a range of different industries, from construction management and advertising to biotechnology and healthcare. To facilitate means "to make an action or process easy or easier," and my job would have been easier in all cases if this book was already available. Why? Well, each of the companies identified some variation of the theme of *Next Generation Leadership* as their top strategic priority. In essence, they all determined that attracting and retaining the best possible young talent was the most important key to their plans to grow, and they all realized that in order to do that effectively they had to evolve their culture to make it more appealing to the next generation. This book shows exactly how that can be done.

The word *generation* comes from the Latin root *generére*, meaning "to beget." The word *beget* is usually used in reference to spawning offspring. It's used a lot in Genesis, but as the dictionary explains, "It can be used to refer to anything that generates something else—for example, an inspiration can beget a brilliant idea." Adam Kingl's inspiration has generated this brilliant work, marrying careful research into generational change with incisive, prescriptive guidance on how to create an optimal culture for young talent to thrive.

This book will be required reading for all my clients in preparation for next year's strategic planning exercises, not just because it is a practical, well-researched guidebook to helping the next generation thrive at work, but also because the book offers a lens into the future of work and leadership.

As an organizational consultant for more than forty years, I've experienced the impact of generational change in corporations, large and small, firsthand. I've worked with regional telephone companies in the aftermath of AT&T's divestiture to help "change bell-shaped heads" and watched with delight as workplaces became more diverse and globally oriented, and less formal and hierarchical. One of my clients who had been a senior manager at AT&T and then Bell Atlantic, which then became Verizon, landed in Seattle, where he was asked to be CEO of a rapidly growing communications technology company. He contacted me in a panic and pleaded: "Please get out here and help me figure out how to connect with these younger folks. Everyone has some kind of piercing, tattoo or mohawk. I feel like I've landed on an alien planet." My client was anxious, but surveys show that the next generation will be the most anxious yet, based on their concern for our fragile environment and the uncertainty in the contemporary workplace. Kingl's research makes it clear, for example, that "with each generation, the number of employers doubles."

Fashions, jargon, and dress codes may change over time, but some things remain constant—and one of those is the need for leadership. Skilled leaders meet people empathically and find a way to appeal to their deeper aspirations, hopes, dreams, and values. The good news is that these are evolving toward greater care toward people and planet.

Legendary economist and Harvard Professor John Kenneth

Galbraith observed that great leaders all have one characteristic in common: the "willingness to confront unequivocally the major anxiety of their people in their time."

Beyond anxiety about the environment and the pressures of changing jobs much more frequently than their predecessors, the next generation of leaders will also deal with what Kingl describes as the "failure of our corporate philosophy of the last century," which he explains as "short-termism and shareholder versus stakeholder orientation." Kingl makes a compelling case that the new generation of leaders are "already reacting against this, and when they assume leadership of our companies, they may usher in a new golden age of the corporate sector working toward the better interests of their customers, employees, and society." This is critical because, as he points out, "our companies are less innovative, agile, and inspirational than their individual employees. In other words, corporate life is less human than it could be."

We are at an inflection point. Previous generations of capitalists just assumed that the planet's resources were unlimited and that the invisible hand of the market would, by focusing solely on shareholder return, provide prosperity for all. But those assumptions are being overturned by our emerging leaders, who, as Kingl shows with detailed research, are reshaping corporate values to be more ecologically astute and human-centered.

Commenting on the Business Roundtable's recent headline-making declaration that the doctrine of shareholder primacy has outlived its usefulness, Johnson & Johnson CEO Alex Gorsky observed, "It isn't an achievement, it's a call to action." Adam Kingl's *Next Generation Leadership* is a superb achievement, and it's also a call to action, offering profound insights and guidance for emerging leaders and for leaders of the previous generations wise enough to avoid the depreciation of their own intellectual capital by engaging in the reverse mentoring process you'll learn about in these pages. Kingl frames all this in the context of a big-picture shift from the shareholder primacy model to a more conscious, regenerative approach to capitalism, and he does so in a way that helps the reader feel engaged. He explains, "Many great movements began with small changes," and then shows how you can begin making those changes now.

—Michael J. Gelb

Author of *How to Think Like Leonardo Da Vinci*

NEXT GENERATION LEADERSHIP

ALTERED STATES OF WORK AND EMPLOYMENT

Today we stand astride a fault line of how commerce may evolve in a global, interconnected society. What's going on, and why now? If we take a very long view, we can observe that capitalism, and its role in society, is challenged and reinvented every one hundred to five hundred years. Feudalism, between the ninth and fifteenth centuries, was replaced by mercantile capitalism, which made way for industrial capitalism in the mid-nineteenth century, which evolved into shareholder capitalism in the twentieth. Capitalism has certainly not been a stagnant system.

When we look even closer, we not only see capitalism as we know it challenged, we must recognize that capitalism today does not manifest in just one form. Scandinavian capitalism certainly looks different from Anglo-Saxon capitalism, yet has created great productivity and social and economic stability; the Scandinavian economies very successfully navigated the last financial crisis. Yes, their citizens pay significantly more taxes than in the United States, but they enjoy a social safety net that reduces both economic and social anxiety. Nordic countries enjoy a healthy work-life balance with longer holidays and shorter workdays. As a result, Finland, Norway, Sweden, and Denmark almost always appear atop the "happiest countries of the world" tables.[1]

Looking eastward, the largest capitalist economy in the world is controlled by the Central Committee of the Chinese Communist Party. Turn back to the West, and the United States is convulsed in debate about the role of government and the degree to which one citizen should contribute to another's security. So, capitalism certainly doesn't follow only one model.

While the wish "May you live in interesting times" is actually a Chinese curse, the reason I am optimistic today is that capitalism actually has a good track record of reinventing itself.[2] We happen to live in one of those inflection points. Shareholder capitalism had its day in the sun, making many executives and investors very wealthy. But every day, employee quality of life has bled out by a thousand paper cuts to pensions, real (adjusted for inflation) incomes, benefits, and work hours.

At the same time, executives from around the world are feeling an unprecedented pressure to reinvent how they lead, learn, operate, structure, incentivize, hire, promote, and communicate. Where is this pressure coming from? Their youngest employees, customers, analysts, and shareholders—the demographic we call Generation Y. Far from being contrary just as a naïve symptom of entitled youth, Generation Y is in fact wise beyond its years. They know, though perhaps subconsciously at times, that business must reflect the needs of its employees, customers, and society in a better way from what we experienced over the past thirty-some years. If capitalism requires reinvention and our societies demand a radical and swift evolution, then the alternative solutions will not come from our gray-haired, wise men in their plush executive suites. The answers may come from Gen Y.

1

IT ALL STARTS
WITH A PATTERN

Each pattern describes a problem which occurs over and over again in our
environment, and then describes the core of the solution to that problem.
—CHRISTOPHER ALEXANDER, human-centered design theorist[1]

A seismic shift has rocked what we previously thought was a
common understanding of work. Because the patterns of
work-life and the employer-employee social contract have
changed over decades rather than days, they have crept up on us.
Today, we are immersed in a new normal, and we find ourselves
scrambling to make sense of what this means for employers, employees, and even the very definition of what it means to work in
the twenty-first century.

One of these patterns has altered so dramatically that if CEOs
from the 1940s and '50s were to step back into the office today,
they would be profoundly shocked. Let me illustrate this particular pattern with my own family's story. When I was growing up in
Silicon Valley, I would visit my grandparents in Wisconsin every
summer. On one of these visits, I remember my ninety-year-old

grandfather ("Grandpa" to you and me) telling me that he retired when he was fifty-five. By the time he was relaying this story
to me, he had been retired for as long as he had worked! Not
only did he work for a single company his entire career, he also
had the *same job* his entire professional life, and this was quite
normal among his contemporaries.

My grandpa's story was surprising to me because I knew that
my parents each had had about three or four employers during
their careers. Curiosity piqued, I started asking my friends and
colleagues if their grandparents and parents had similar employment histories, and this pattern turned out to be almost always
true for their families as well. So here was an intriguing circum-
stance: Our grandparents typically had one employer while our
parents had three to four.

As I entered my thirties, I was still intrigued with this shift in
the number of employers among different generations. If current patterns continue, most of my friends and colleagues belonging to Generation X (born between approximately 1961 and
1981) will probably have between six to eight employers during
their lifetimes. Entering my forties, I began asking my youngest
colleagues, Generation Y (born between approximately 1982 and
2004), about their career histories and discovered that if their
typical rate of job changes were to continue, they would have
fifteen to sixteen employers in their lifetimes. Even more dramatically, quite a few of my Generation Y colleagues think nothing of
changing jobs every year or two: Acquire some experience or
development and move on.

In this respect, a pattern emerges that is both sparklingly clear
and breathtakingly exponential in its inexorable escalation. With
each generation, the number of employers doubles.

Generation	Born Between	Average # of Employers in Lifetime
Silent Generation[2]	1925–1942	1–2
Baby Boomers	1943–1960	3–4
Generation X	1961–1981	6–8
Generation Y	1982–2004	15–16
Generation Z	2005+	???

We have to ask ourselves, should this trend continue, if our children and grandchildren in Generation Z are going to have thirty to thirty-two employers in their lifetime. When will this trend reach a breaking point? I'll return to this theme later.

This phenomenon was fascinating, and further research indicated the trend was in fact more widely true, not just within my own observation. A recent Gallup survey reported that 21 percent of our youngest employees changed jobs within one year, more than three times the rate of their older counterparts, costing the U.S. economy $30.5 billion annually.[3] What's behind that erosion of constancy and reliability in the workforce?

In 2009, I was the director of an executive education open-enrollment program at London Business School called the Emerging Leaders Program. I realized that the participants were a gold mine of research data to help me answer these questions. They were almost all squarely within Generation Y, most in their twenties. I decided to issue a survey to this group and removed any respondent who was outside this generation, which was a very small number.

What was most exciting was that, by virtue of their companies' nominating and sponsoring their attendance in this program, this group of students was a fine example of the future leaders of their companies and industries. This was much better than a generic sample of their generation. If these participants were the "high potentials" in their companies, then this group might tell us not only about their generation's attitudes toward work, management, and leadership, but their opinions would be strong leading indicators of how companies *might be led in the future.*

GIVE ME DATA!

I had my dataset: two cohorts per year, surveyed while on the program over five years, and representing forty-four countries[4] across five continents. I followed the survey with interviewing many of the participants to delve deeper into their answers, which gave me qualitative insights.

The first aspect I wished to explore was: If Generation Y themselves are consciously mobile in their employment, do they *expect* to move around with such unprecedented rapidity? Therefore, my first question in the survey was, "How long do you expect to stay with any given employer?" In other words, "When you join a company, what does the little voice in the back of your head tell you about how long you would expect to be there?" The answers demonstrated that these young managers did indeed enter a workplace with no desire to be a "company man or woman," pursuing a job for life.

How long do you expect to stay with any given employer?

11+ years	5 percent
6–10 years	5 percent
3–5 years	53 percent
1–2 years	37 percent

Ninety percent of the participants reported that they fully anticipate leaving an employer within five years of joining it. More than a third believe they will leave within twenty-four months. Other research from the World Economic Forum indicates an even more sobering statistic—that 69 percent of workers aged eighteen to twenty-four will leave their employer within a year. I was shocked that the percent of answers in my survey did not in-

crease one jot from "11+" years to the "6–10 years" responses—
that the very idea of staying somewhere for more than five years
seemed practically inconceivable. We will explore more fully in
chapter 3 some of the reasons behind this destruction of the old
employee-employer social contract, and that indeed both sides
can take credit (or blame?) for this massive shift.

There is another critical consideration for managers if employees are going to leave with such casual haste. Namely, how can we
"exit" our most valuable employees with the expectation that we
can attract them back to the organization at a later date? In this
environment where loyalty can no longer be expected, how can
employers still gain some advantage over their competitors in the
talent war? We'll delve deep into this issue in chapters 3 and 4.

My next question in the survey attempted to scope where employee loyalty lay, if indeed it can be found anywhere. How much
does the company brand—its mission, vision, and values—come
into play, or is employee engagement among Gen Yers more
aligned to one's immediate, day-to-day experience with colleagues? The survey suggests the latter.

Do you feel more loyal to your team or to your organization?

Team	54 percent
Organization	46 percent

On the one hand, one might think, "The results are pretty
close, so this is not so significant." I would argue that we can just
as easily flip that reasoning on its head and say, "The fact that
more than half of Gen Y employees say they are more loyal to their
colleagues than to their company is, in itself, hugely important."

Many corporations today spend inordinate amounts of time
and money on their "employer brand," when in fact they might
just need to turn their efforts more locally to the intimate environments of their myriad teams, who create and deliver value
for customers and provide job satisfaction for the team members themselves, not only for a "job well done" but for being part
of a community of friends and colleagues. This conclusion is

consistent with one of Gallup's studies, which found that a key dimension of an engaged organization is that its members can honestly say, "I have a best friend at work."[5] Even if we do not interact face-to-face with our colleagues every day, the behaviors and habits of social media have pivoted our employees' focal point onto their relationships with their team members versus their institutions. I will discuss this shift in much more detail in chapter 5.

What are the factors, then, that attract high-flying Gen Ys to a given company? What would help to engage them and perhaps keep them a little bit longer? In seeking answers, my next question in the survey attempted to reveal what the most important employer benefits might be and if these are different from what many organizations expect to emphasize. In this case, I asked the survey-takers to rank their top three criteria from a list, and the ranking was weighted. In other words, an answer ranked as the "number one" most important factor was weighted more important than an answer rated number two or three.

The list of factors from which people chose was a mix of traditional and untraditional, financial and nonfinancial benefits and characteristics. Here's the list of factors in alphabetical order:

What matters most to you in selecting an employer?
- ▶ Benefits package
- ▶ CEO's reputation
- ▶ Corporate social responsibility
- ▶ Development opportunities
- ▶ Openness to innovation
- ▶ Organizational culture
- ▶ Performance-based bonus
- ▶ Share price performance
- ▶ Work-life balance

The answers represent a dramatic shift from previous expectations—not a single one of the top three most popular answers was a financial benefit.

The third most popular answer was "development opportunities." But to avoid any confusion, when I followed up with the survey-takers in conversation, they were very clear that a development opportunity does not have to be a promotion. Indeed, one might assume that if the typical Gen Y employee is only going to stay for about two years, then the only way to keep that employee is to promote him or her every eighteen to twenty-four months. That is, of course, completely unrealistic; there just aren't enough rungs on the corporate ladder. But if employers stop translating "development opportunity" as "promotion," then a whole array of valuable offers reveals themselves: mentorships, coaching, executive education, more important projects or client work, collaboration with more senior staff, and the list goes on. None of these opportunities are as expensive as promotions, and most have no additional cost at all. I will look at these "benefits" and how to make them work more effectively in chapter 8.

The second most popular answer to this "benefits" question was "organizational culture." This really comes as little surprise, as more time and attention in business and academia have turned to culture or "what it means to work here." Part of the attention is due to a disagreement, or at least a disconnect, in what companies and leaders can do about their culture to enhance performance and engagement. Far too many organizations turn their focus, or that of their expensive consultants, to telling a good story—in carefully crafting a mission, vision, and values statement to delight and dazzle their stakeholders and shareholders. Short of authenticity, or of making the connection between words and behaviors, these exercises are little more than propaganda pieces. In chapter 4, I will share some case studies of companies that have genuinely shifted their cultures into sustainable, competitive advantages by moving beyond superficial word-crafting.

The number one most popular answer to what Gen Y employees seek from their employer or potential employer is "work-life balance."[6] This topic is one of the most contentious among the generations. I hear older generations bemoaning that their young employees "don't work as hard as we do [or perhaps *did?*]." Or, "We had to bust our tails to work our way up the corporate ladder. Now it's their turn, and they don't understand how to get ahead." On the other hand, Gen Yers are observing that their bosses expect "pointless, endless face time" in the office, which has nothing to do with productivity or achieving one's objectives.

My observation is that there is a misunderstanding here. When we say "work-life balance," the older generations hear that as a "when" (or hours of work) issue, while Gen Ys hear a "where" (or location of work) issue. In other words, according to their bosses, Gen Ys are working fewer hours. According to Gen Y, they are not working fewer hours; they are working anywhere, anytime, rather than nine to five, Monday to Friday, in the office. This first wholly digital generation simply recognizes that being shackled to a desk does not necessarily produce the best outcomes for the individual or for the company, that technology allows one to work from home, on weekends, across time zones, and so on. Since we never really stop working, then let's finally put to bed the myth that face time in the office is a fair indicator of employee output. I will explore virtual work and how to maximize its productivity in chapter 7.

There are other elements in this survey, as well as insights from my interviews with executives and high potentials in many vanguard companies, that reinforce that our world of work is changing forever. Members of our youngest generation in the workforce clearly hold different paradigms than those of previous generations. This has little to do with life stage, that somehow "We were just like Gen Y, and they will come around to our way of thinking as they get older, marry, have children." There are macro-trends, which I will illustrate in the next chapter, that have permanently altered how people entering the workforce view careers, work-life, and leadership.

If we can make some simple changes to how we manage Generation Y, who will compose 75 percent of the global workforce by 2025,[7] then the advantages for those forward-looking organizations will be deep and lasting. First, those companies will attract the best talent, keep them longer, and in some cases attract that talent to return later in their careers. Second, those companies will connect with customers and shareholders, comprising more Gen Ys with every passing day, more easily and deeply. Third, these organizations will pioneer new and more resonant models of leadership that will fundamentally alter the nature of work and the nature of the commercial enterprise. Finally, our children and grandchildren face far different career paths from our own. We serve them better by fully comprehending the environment in which they will embark upon their professional lives. The stakes couldn't be much higher. Shall we begin?

2

THE OBSESSION AND DISCONTENT WITH GENERATIONS

People try to put us down
Just because we get around
Things they do look awful cold
I hope I die before I get old
—THE WHO, "My Generation"[1]

The study of generational theory is often misconstrued and made worse by those who define generations only by the span of years in which they were born and not their contexts. It's quick and easy but also far too simplistic and leads to misconceptions and accusations: If a generation's character is solely a function of years of birth, then what's the point of defining them at all? Surely, they're all the same in the end, and the differences we see at any point are just functions of life stage?

I've delivered dozens of speeches on generations over the past few years. These were useful exercises in stress testing my ideas—highly recommended! I hear the "It's just a life stage" argument more than any other by the skeptics of generational study. The quickest retort I have to the naysayers is that if every generation is ultimately the same as any other, then their patterns of education, labor, and retirement would be identical as they age. If they are in fact different, then there must be something more going on.

Of course, I'm not saying that the generations are biologically different, that there is somehow a different genetic code. The differences are those of nurture rather than nature. A generation, with all its strengths and maddening quirks, is shaped by the epoch or context in which it is raised.[2] I'm defining "epoch" as the political situation, economic state, dominant parenting style, and national and world attitudes that dominated each generation's developmental years. This explains why the number of birth years is not exactly the same from generation to generation. Epochs have a funny habit of changing at different rates. Once many of the dominant paradigms across a range of spectra change significantly, then we draw a line and begin to define a new generation.

This concept is not new; more than sixty-five years ago, sociologist Karl Mannheim[3] argued that people are shaped by their shared experiences. Almost thirty years ago, the authors and historians Neil Howe and William Strauss[4] built on Mannheim's hypothesis that the similarities of people within a generation can be attributed to social change. While their research focused on the United States going back to the sixteenth century, Howe and Strauss accurately summarized that, as a generation is influenced by sometimes subtly and sometimes radically different values, the result can be confusion and tension among the generations. So, empathy helps as well as simply recognizing that if context during formative years is different among generations, then we cannot assume that attitudes toward lives, careers, and the world would be identical.

A more valid challenge to generational theory that I hear when delivering my keynotes is that if the social context is entirely different in one country versus another, then the generational characteristics, even if people are born in the same years, must also be different. I do have sympathy with this argument and agree up to a point. It is worth acknowledging that different countries will have experienced the shifts that define generations at slightly, or sometimes dramatically, different times. For example, we could argue that the birth years defining the generations of the twentieth century in the United States are a little earlier than those defining the same generations in the United Kingdom. However, the differences are insignificant enough that they are not worth nitpicking, else we can't see the forest for the trees. Until the advent of the twenty-first century, I would agree that the generational definitions I use here applied more toward the West, OECD (Organisation for Economic Cooperation and Development) countries, and most of the dominant research applied even more specifically to the U.S. population. Political forces and beliefs ebb and flow, and this creates nuances among the same generation in different countries. But the interconnectedness of the globe, supercharged by the internet, implies that we have more values and beliefs in common with those from other countries than at any other time in the history of our planet.

Other changes, such as digital adoption itself, are far too widespread to claim that they are anything other than ubiquitous. Even in many of the most remote and economically disadvantaged regions of the world, we observe that digital and mobile technology is pervasive. In rural India, for example, because subsistence farmers have access to mobile technology allowing them to see real-time market prices, they can benefit from warehousing their surplus grain and maize rather than selling it too cheaply, adding 20–30 percent to their income.[5] Truly, we can no longer say that digital or mobile adoption is anything other than global.

However, we may certainly conclude that digital adoption occurred at different ages among Baby Boomers, Gen X, Gen Y, and Gen Z. While all four generations may be perfectly comfortable living in the digital age today, the fact that one generation learned to be digital mid-career, the next generation accustomized to digital as young adults, the third generation grew up amid exponential digital adoption, and the fourth was *born into digital* makes a huge difference in how these segments view themselves and their world. For example, Gen Y grew up with almost instant and complete access to news happening anywhere in the world. As a result, and combined with other factors such as cheaper travel, they are more likely to be empathetic toward crises occurring abroad and to want to contribute to solutions. Geographic distance is almost trivial, and therefore Gen Y is the first to be a truly global community, where it is natural and simple to connect with individuals and groups from almost any country any time. This is significant in terms of how Gen Y views world charities, politics in other countries, religions, and even where they envision living in the future.

Of course, one cannot say that these conclusions about generations apply fully and equally to every individual within any given generation. In characterizing such huge populations, we must inevitably generalize. Therefore, I have no doubt that you can think of one or even many people for whom the generational claims I make in this book do not apply. That's absolutely fine. The point is that to have a little more clarity about trends and patterns can only help us to be proactive and confident in terms of how we navigate through the hazy fug of preparing for the future.

Similarly, when I've delivered speeches on this topic, I encounter people in genuine angst because they were born in the years dividing two generations. Their concern is typically in the category of, "I don't feel as if I belong to one generation or the other. Help!" The simple answer is that there will always be individuals whose outlooks on life may more closely resemble those of different generations than their own, and these people are understandably more commonly found among those born in the "border years." There's no problem with that. Belonging to a generation does not *require* you to identify with it. The emotion that I've observed in the audience during these keynotes speaks to our deep human instinct to belong and the unsettled feeling, even foreboding, when we don't have an affinity for our prescribed tribe. To those who may experience this sense of disconnection, I would say that we can find connection with communities by other definitions, too (our hobbies, faiths, passions, etc.), and we also can give ourselves permission to belong to two tribes. For example, someone born in 1980 might think, "I have the healthy institutional skepticism of Gen X and the entrepreneurial drive of Gen Y."

We must also acknowledge that the differences we observe in the mind-sets between generations occur gradually, like the changing of the seasons. It is not as if one person born in 1981 would have a completely different outlook from someone born in 1982 just because these birth years are roughly the dividing point between two generations. We who study generations use bands of birth years to distinguish one from another, but their differences cannot be so finely cut with razor-like accuracy. Since social contexts change over longer periods of time, there is some overlap of social, parental, political, and economic trends. So, putting skepticism aside and content that we may or may not personally identify precisely with the generations defined herein, let's explore their stories.

THE GENERATIONS

For ease of reference, I have outlined here in a simple table some of the most significant contexts in which the generations in the workforce today, and the coming generation, were raised. As you read this, consider the implications of what the members of each generation value, how they view the world, how they think about work and careers, and in what ways they have been supported and disappointed in their formative years.

•   •   •

	Born Between	Conflict	Digital	Economy	Institutional Support	Parenting	Children Have . . .
Baby Boomers	1943–1960	World War II, Cold War	Analog	Boom	Strongly supported	"Train your baby," traditional parent roles	Chores, after-school jobs at younger ages
Gen X	1961–1981	Vietnam War, Cold War, period of relative peace in the 1990s, Gulf Wars	Begin in analog, grow into and lay the foundations of the digital world	Boom and bust cycles	Questioned, counter-culture movement in 1960s	Flexible and affectionate, more mothers working, more parents divorcing, less supervision, raised on TV, "the MTV generation"	Some chores, after-school jobs in older ages
Gen Y	1982–2004	Gulf Wars, Terrorism	Digital is normal, "answers are found on the internet," social media community	Great Recession	Strongly questioned	Unwavering support, no such thing as failure, both parents usually work	Activities, very structured and regimented
Gen Z	2005–Now	Terrorism	Digital natives	Growth	Questioned, particularly government	Strong family affinity, self-reliant	Projects, more leeway from parents[6]

BABY BOOMERS

Baby Boomers are as voluminous as they are influential, the children of servicemen and women returning from World War II and essentially, well, having lots of babies! After the hell of war, Boomers grew up in a world where they watched their parents[7] desperately rebuilding and retrenching their beloved institutions (organized religion, corporations, governments) in order to rediscover emotional, financial, and political security. For this generation, working for one employer for many years represented security in an age for which the recent past had very little: loyalty, discipline, and strong identity with the company and its ethos. "The IBM Man" (for it was in its day still more likely to be a man in full-time work) became a common term in this generation for the lifelong employee, working up the ranks and rewarded for tenure and tenacity. As writer Rich Cohen so aptly characterized: "They were the biggest . . . most free-spending market the planet had ever known. What they wanted filled the shelves, and what fills the shelves is our history."[8] Management style was dominantly command-and-control, influenced by the strongest social organization of that era—the military. Security in retirement was an expected reward for decades of graft and following orders, and a Defined Benefit pension would allow one the surety of a fixed income for all the years of one's remaining life. After many years of rapprochement with institutions, it was only in the counterculture movement of the late 1960s that we began to see the pendulum swing back toward rejection of the suburban "slow death" and rediscovery of the individualistic spirit—the knell of the Baby Boomer generation and the harbinger of Generation X.

GENERATION X

I must admit at this point that I have always been slightly disappointed with the term Generation X. It doesn't give us much room for the future—where do we go after Y and Z? It's like naming an art movement "modernist." Where can we go after "post-modernist"? But Generation X entrenched itself in the popular vocabulary, and so it shall be. Funny enough, the name Generation X first appeared in a photo essay by Robert Capa in the 1950s about young adults growing up in the shadow of World War II, but "X" would only stick after author Douglas Copeland published his novel titled *Generation X: Tales for an Accelerated Culture*,[9] whose heroes were young adults growing up in the 1980s. "X" referred to the idea of a placeholder; in other words, "unknown."[10]

As a member of this generation myself, I recall hearing the term Generation X for the first time in college. The context was, "We don't understand what this generation is about, what they're thinking, what they value, what contribution they will make." Gen X has also been called an "in-between generation," squeezed between two tremendous populations, the Boomers and Ys, pressing on either side.[11] This lends further credence to the thought that as an "unknown" or "cipher" generation, the simple fact of their smaller population indicated that their contribution might be minor.

I do not add my support to this view. Gen X certainly has made significant contributions, including building in no small manner the social and corporate infrastructure of the digital economy. As the last complete generation that clacked on a typewriter, dialed a rotary phone, and used a card catalog at the library, one could argue that Generation X architected, consciously and unconsciously, the manner, habit, and ethos of what it would mean to live in the digital age.

Perhaps the ambivalent assessment of Xs twenty years ago partially derived from the observation that Xs were raised on television and video games. Both parents were pushed into the workforce as wages failed to keep up with inflation. The term "latchkey kids" became commonplace for this generation—children returning from school and letting themselves into an empty house, kept company by the TV until their parents returned from work. The familial instability was exacerbated by an increasing rate of divorce among these same parents.

At the same time, Gen Xs watched their parents cope with a stormy economic climate of boom and bust from the turbo-charged eighties to the recession and unemployment of the early nineties. Pensions were ruined or raided as corporations sought liquidity to stay afloat. No longer was a pension a "salary in retirement" but a pot of money that may or may not pay for one's retirement until death. University tuition rose far above inflation, forcing Xs to remain in student loan debt for much longer, and the cost has included indefinitely putting off owning property or planning retirement.

For Gen Xs, neither family nor employer was a trusted institution that would look out for you in good times and in bad.[12] This mind-set may have been the seed for the higher turnover of Gen Xs in the workforce, as they never had their parents' deeper trust that their institutions would reward their loyalty.

GENERATION Y

Now we come to that most bewildering generation—the Ys. I am intentionally avoiding using the term "Millennials," because I've heard some confuse "Millennial" to mean "those born in the new Millennium." I will therefore remain consistent with Howe and Strauss's term "Generation Y," but substitute "Millennial" if you wish now that we've established the same working definition.

Gen Y grew up with the most traumatic economic convulsion of the past eighty years—the Great Recession of 2007–09. While this event wasn't as severe as the Great Depression of 1929–39, its impact on this generation's sense of security and trust was fundamental. Observing their parents losing their jobs, hushed conversations behind half-closed doors about money, banks shuttering their doors, pension plans decimated, their houses foreclosed, Gen Ys' attitude toward economic security was formed, molded by hard experience: Companies will not look after you for life. So as soon as you have acquired what you sought from one employer, move on to the next to help you take the next step in your career.

As terrorism became more prevalent during Gen Ys' child-hood, what appears as impatience with employers may also be viewed through a different lens as seizing the present, since we may not be here tomorrow. As bleak as that view may appear, their environment reinforced the Gen Ys' *carpe diem* philosophy of work and life. It became quite obvious in the late noughties that betting on the long term was for suckers. For Generation Y, the Great Recession was what academic Warren Bennis would call a "crucible of experience" or "a transformative experience through which an individual comes to a new or altered sense of identity."[13]

An interesting by-product of this paradigm is that Gen Ys seek immediate and rich experiences from work.[14] It's not, "How is my company building my skills and professional profile over the next ten years?" It's, "How is my company helping me *now*? How is my identity and value enhanced by the tasks put to me?" This mental model is not only true in the workplace but in leisure as well. A recent lifestyle survey revealed that Generation Y prefers rich experiences (we might even say "recreational crucibles") over luxury or comfort escapes.[15] In other words, "How do my holidays also enhance my sense of self, my courage, my empathy, and my identity as a self-reliant person?"

Now that we've painted the picture of the social context that shaped Gen Ys' formative years, let's explore three macro-trends that indicate how and why the world of work is fundamentally different for younger employees today.

1. Significantly longer forecasted life spans offer young people an uncertain retirement but more opportunity to explore and experience different jobs and even different careers.[16]
2. Typical retirement plans today also contribute to future uncertainty and are dramatically unattractive in their ability to retain employees.
3. The proliferation of contract work calls into question how we perceive "our job."

The first macro-trend is that our youngest employees know they will live much longer and enjoy a higher quality of life for more of their older age. London Business School professors Lynda Gratton and Andrew Scott argue that young people today who were born in developed countries have a greater than 50 percent chance to live to be more than one hundred years old.[17] As this fact becomes apparent to Gen Y, they will take a much more flexible, evolutionary, and personal approach to their careers than that of generations past.

Increasing life span, the daunting challenge of financing a long retirement, and a shorter period of morbidity (or disability in older age) mean that the classic retirement age of sixty-five is quickly becoming anomalous. Therefore, if graduates expect that they can and will work from, say, twenty-two to eighty-two, they have huge scope to reinvent themselves professionally several times over. For example, one could earn a degree, train, and work as a doctor for thirty years, then earn a degree, train, and work as a lawyer for another thirty years. Forget loyalty to a single company—Generation Y, with the luxury of time, doesn't even have to be loyal to a single career.

The second macro-trend is related to the first. Because of longer life, companies over the past twenty-five years or so have had to radically change their pension plans in order for both the retirement fund and the corporate balance sheet to be sustainable in the long term.

The most significant change has been the switch from Defined Benefit (DB) to Defined Contribution (DC) pensions. A DB pension is typically correlated to one's final salary on retirement. The retiree earns a fraction of the final year's salary (the fraction is a function of the number of years of service) guaranteed for every year of retirement until death, and the surviving spouse often earns a fraction of that payment, too, until death. While this final salary annual payment is usually adjusted for inflation, it is fixed, hence a "Defined Benefit." Obviously, this is a hugely desirable pension plan because it is guaranteed retirement income regardless of how long one lives.

Like all pensions and public schemes, such as Social Security, the plan only funds itself if the revenue into the pension plan from current employees exceeds the outgoing costs—the retirees drawing their pension payouts. While average life expectancy was in one's early seventies in 1980, the total number of retirees drawing a pension was controlled by people dying on average no more than a few years after retiring (sorry to sound a morbid tone). Today, average life expectancy in the developed world is more than ten years higher.[18] So the DB pension plan doesn't balance anymore—the outgoings exceed the incomings. To make the plan soluble yet retain the final salary scheme would require employers and employees to contribute exponentially more to the pension every month, far more than most can stomach.

In response to this growing pension crisis, companies have adjusted their plans to become DC schemes. They're really not "pensions" at all in the literal sense of the word. They may be known as "retirement funds" or more obscurely 401(k)s or 403(b)s in the United States. In these plans, employees pay into investment products, which operate like mutual funds, often with some employer-matching payments. These plans are portfolios of assets of sometimes one, sometimes multiple, asset classes (equities, bonds, commodities, mutual funds, etc.). In this manner, the company has insulated itself from the risk of not knowing how long its retirees will live. The problem is that the company has now passed that risk on to its employees. The employee also assumes the risk that the value of the retirement fund might decline if the investments don't perform well; the nightmare scenario is a market crash just before retiring.

During the 1980s and '90s, the decline in pension coverage went largely unnoticed. This is because large companies tried to alter their plans gradually. Dramatic changes to the pension plans of Fortune 100 companies would have immediately drawn the attention of the media. But newer, smaller companies weren't even offering pensions at all. As these small companies grew into big ones (Dell, Home Depot), traditional pensions became less commonplace. U.S. tax legislation launched 401(k)s in 1978, which really gained traction in the 1980s during a great upswing in the stock market, making them appear to be very effective. But was it correlation or causation? It is possible that the sudden influx of retirement savings into such investment funds helped to boost the equity market upswing. The early success of the 401(k) coupled with the slowly creeping death of traditional pension plans meant that most Americans did not mourn the loss of the final salary scheme or pay much attention to the difference between the two plans. However, an important point was lost in those early years—that 401(k)s were intended to supplement rather than replace pensions.[19]

That has become a massive problem because, while there is flexibility in terms of how much retirees choose to withdraw from the DC scheme, 401(k), and so on,[20] at any one time, the total value of that fund is finite. So, if retirees withdraw all the money in their plan and they're still alive, they had better have another source of income. How much should we be investing in our retirement if we're going to live decades longer than our great-grandparents? Some estimates state that a middle-aged person should be investing at least 20–25 percent of their income to finance their retirement—far more than most individuals today are able or willing to contribute. The conclusion most of us must inevitably reach: We will simply have to delay our retirement.[21]

Gen Ys have already come to this conclusion, albeit unwillingly and pessimistically. Eighty percent of American adults under age thirty believe their generation will be "much worse off" than their parents' generation because of not only poor pension plans but the declining sustainability of Social Security and Medicare.[22] We're facing a perfect storm of longevity, disintegrating pensions, and declining Social Security (or "national insurance," in some countries) that forces Generation Y to consider the unpalatable truth that their old age will be more uncertain and difficult than old age has been for almost a century.

How a company typically experiences this pessimism is through a lack of constancy among their employees. The company, however, has done itself no favors since it has not softened the economic woe on its people. While a DB pension plan rewards an employee for staying with the company for as long as possible, a DC plan removes that incentive, perhaps the most significant material reward for loyalty. In fact, most DC plans today allow the employee to carry the investments wherever they go.[23] Therefore, the employer has lost its historically most powerful tool for retaining talent. Is it any wonder, then, that companies are finding it difficult to keep young employees? Corporations really have only themselves to blame! While corporations' reasons for changing pension schemes were perhaps necessary, it's perfectly understandable that demonstrably weaker pensions contribute to the incentive for employees to look out for themselves, jumping more readily to the next immediate, valuable opportunity or experience.

The pension trouble is compounded by the fact that salaries have on average not appreciated in line with inflation.[24] For example, real wage growth in the United Kingdom has been close to zero since 2010. A recent survey revealed, furthermore, that 57 percent of British people believe that the young will have a worse standard of life than their parents.[25] The situation is actually worse in the United States. For example, in real terms adjusted for inflation, the U.S. federal minimum wage has slipped from $10.90 per hour in 1960 to $7.25 in 2015, a drop of a third.[26] Consider that our employees at the bottom of the corporate ladder are typically earning the lowest salaries, and we have yet another reason why Generation Y feels little to no compunction to reward their employers with long service. In fact, the alternatives become more attractive by the year: Either job-hop with abandon or go it alone.

The third macro-trend is the widespread use of contract work. In order to reduce the long-term hit to their balance sheets, enhance flexibility, and protect themselves from greater pension liability, companies are relying increasingly on short-term workers. The signal to the labor market is that corporations do not value long-term commitment; in fact, they are making long-term commitments more difficult to make, even among willing employees.

There is perhaps an unintended consequence: Gen Y has gotten used to the independence and empowerment that come with a "portfolio" career. That's the silver lining for a generation that is much larger than X in terms of sheer numbers, fighting for the limited number of full-time, low-paying, permanent jobs. As opposed to resigning themselves to the futility of this situation, Gen Y is taking up the mantle of self-reliance by other means that their great-grandparents during the Great Depression had role modelled. As a contractor, the young high-flier can work for the highest bidder, accept only the most interesting work, cherry-pick contracts with those companies that treat them well, and build diverse experiences (international, nonprofit, different industries and functions) into his or her résumé.

Yes, there are disadvantages, too, including that contractors are completely reliant on their own will, discipline, and resources to finance their retirement. At the moment, a whopping 68 percent of working-age Americans are not participating in an employer-sponsored retirement plan.[27] In the United Kingdom, the number of self-employed who are putting savings into a pension has fallen precipitously from 1.1 million in 2001 to just 380,000 in 2015.[28] On the other hand, there are certainly many in the gig economy who report that being the master of one's fate can be a marvelous place to be. But at what price down the line?

GENERATION Z

While this book focuses on Generation Y, it's worthwhile to peer into the future a bit deeper to see how our children and grandchildren in Generation Z, those not yet in the workforce, might shape our world. This is the first digitally native generation, never knowing a time without the internet and mobile devices. There are numerous videos on YouTube of toddlers trying to swipe or enlarge the pictures in magazines with their fingers.[29] The inevitable video title: "To a baby, a magazine is an iPad that doesn't work."

If we look at the older band of Gen Z, another digital trend is the decline in email use, displaced by social apps[30] such as WhatsApp and Yammer. A couple years ago, I attended the Peter Drucker Forum, an annual conference in Vienna that explores management innovation. A panel of forty- and fifty-year-old "gurus" was discussing how email usage, especially among the young, is eroding deeper discourse in the workplace and in society more broadly. A young student in the audience stood up and said, "If you think we use email, you really don't understand us at all." An audible whoosh of surprise and shock exhaled through the hall, as it suddenly dawned on the panel how distorted their view of this generation was.

Early indicators are that Gen Zs continue our journey toward a more inclusive and tolerant society, as 81 percent of Gen Zs report a statistically significant improvement in having "friends of a different race" compared to 69 percent of Gen Ys. Seventy-seven percent of Gen Zs have no issue with marrying someone of a different race, versus 66 percent of Ys. Fifty-nine percent of Zs have "friends of a different sexual orientation" versus 53 percent of Ys, and 66 percent favor marriage equality compared to 58 percent of Gen Ys.[31]

While our children have always represented our hope for the future, I suspect that it has been more than half a century since we have hoped with such ferocity that our youngest will bring greater civility, community, objectivity, tolerance, and empathy to society. We can but hope.

INSIGHTS TO ACTIONS
One Thing You Can Do Monday Morning

I attempt to stay firmly and proudly in the practitioner camp in terms of my perspective and my professional life. Research is a tremendous gift to humankind in our search for truth, particularly in this age of so-called fake news. Could I say anything less, given I've spent most of my life studying in and working for universities? But for the realm in which I operate in terms of my clients, those in the business world, the most important question to answer is: "What do we do with this insight? How does this move me or my organization forward?" So, I will finish every chapter hereafter with a suggested application of the insight from that section. In this way, this book resembles an executive education program in miniature, a dialogue that is ultimately action-focused rather than hypothetical musing.

For this chapter's activity, my suggestion is first to understand what the demographic pattern is in your enterprise. Identify what percent of your employees are Generation Y, Generation X, and Baby Boomer. Repeat this exercise every few years, not only because the composition will change, but because, in just a few years, Generation Zs will be applying for jobs with you. The insight from this activity should be worthwhile in that the percent of Gen Ys in your company will act as an "urgency index" for how quickly your company may need to consider and adopt some of the recommendations from this book.

The cost of not acting in relation to the alteration in your demographics, and more important your internal paradigms, will be felt at minimum in your organization's ability to recruit, retain, and engage your people. If you actually want to quantify this cost, ask your human resources department what the average length of service was for an employee twenty years ago and compare that to today. As already established, Gen Y is going to stay for a shorter amount of time on average than previous generations, but the goal is to lengthen that time, even by a couple of years.

In each year, what is the additional number of people the company must recruit as a result of the higher voluntary turnover? Then take the average cost to recruit and orient a new employee and multiply that figure by the additional number of people from your previous question. There you have a quick and fairly accurate cost (and there are other costs for sure!) to the company in not adapting to the changing perspective of a radically different workforce. If you agree that your organization needs to transform to respond and thrive in a new environment, then this exercise should provide you with plenty of ammunition to make your case for what's at stake if the company were to change nothing.

3

LOYALTY ISN'T AS RELIABLE AS IT USED TO BE

Maybe we're loyal and maybe we're not
Yeah, we got our secrets, but where does it stop? . . .
If we're always searching for a life that's perfect
How we ever gonna know just what we got?
—PALOMA FAITH, "Loyal"[1]

In just eighty years, employee loyalty seismically shifted from staying with one employer (and if you were living during the Great Depression, why wouldn't you stay with whoever would hire you?) to 90 percent of our younger workers moving to another company every four to five years, and more than a third in two years or fewer. You may recall these statistics from chapter 1; there are other data points that corroborate this shocking result. A Deloitte survey of more than ten thousand Gen Ys, roughly half from developed markets and half from emerging markets across thirty-six countries, asked, "How long would you stay with your current employer before leaving to join a new organization or do something different?" Forty-three percent responded that they would leave within two years.[2]

As loyalty, or rather the lack thereof, among Gen Ys to their employers is often the first characteristic that organizations identify as different and problematic, one might ask if there's an upside to this situation. Why has loyalty eroded, and how might companies adjust their own behavior to reflect this new reality?

The first step in closing the rift is for employers to admit that they have contributed to the problem in the first place. It's not Gen Y "irresponsibility," but companies' unraveling, stitch by stitch, all the factors that bound their employees to their enterprises. First, as we have explored, typical, annual pension payout used to be a function of years of service. The longer one worked for his or her company, the harder it would be to walk away until retirement. Today, Defined Contribution pensions benefit the employees in that they are mobile, but expose them to market decline and the risk of running out of income near the end of a long life. DC pensions favor the employers in insulating them from market volatility and the lengthening life spans of their retirees but increasing employee turnover without the traditional golden handcuffs of final salary pensions.

If Gen X has had to reevaluate its concept of retirement as more distant and difficult to attain, Gen Y is almost dismissing retirement entirely. Realists acknowledge that they cannot expect to have sufficient finances to retire at sixty-five and will work indefinitely. Optimists hope they can fund their later years with at least part-time work into their eighties or nineties. But longer life expectancy, better health, and activity in older years means that Gen Ys are not only reevaluating the concept of retirement, they are also reconsidering the definition of a career. They simply have more time to explore company experiences, career options and changes (even in later life), personal development, and more and varied career stages than previous generations enjoyed. Adaptability to renew and even reinvent their careers, continuous development, and access to more senior, interesting, and supportive managers and clients are the new currency that employers may spend to attract and retain their top, young talent (even if it's for a few more years versus for life). In other words, if companies can no longer afford pensions and other material benefits to enhance their employer value, they can deliver much more on personal and career development to make up at least some of the deficit.[3]

In addition to weak pensions, Gen Y graduate roles are also less attractive because employers have been lazy about making them compelling. This is at least partially due to Generation Y's population being much larger than Generation X's, and so employers have taken the view that one should be grateful to have a job at all. Well, Gen Ys see it differently. Since they will live a long time and because development and the capacity to reinvent are so dear to them, Gen Ys simply acquire the experience or "badge" for their CV from one company and then look elsewhere for the next challenge.

Because quickly acquiring the badges of notable experiences is cherished in this environment, Gen Ys have also redesigned how they can achieve those badges more efficiently. Whereas Gen Xs look forward to a portfolio career of part-time work, projects, consulting, and nonexecutive positions in their twilight years, Gen Ys have embraced the portfolio career as a realistic option from the very beginning of their work lives—there's more risk but, at the same time, more control over selecting one's projects and colleagues.

A study conducted by software company Intuit in 2010 predicted that more than 40 percent of the U.S. workforce will be freelancers by 2020. That's up from 30 percent in 2006 and represents more than sixty million contractors, temporary employees, and the self-employed.[4] Employers now have a choice to make about how they collaborate with the densely inhabited population of portfolio-career Gen Ys. These choices come with different implications for what our organizational charts may look like. A traditional company's organizational chart might resemble something like this, admittedly dramatically simplified:

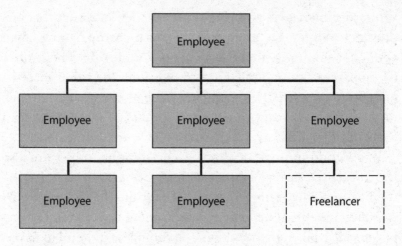

Yet if some of the brightest, most imaginative young talents choose to work for themselves, organizations may consider how and if they can pivot to an architecture that would have appeared anathema to most twentieth-century human resource departments—an organizational design filled with freelancers accountable for the myriad projects through which most companies now organize their work. For additional complexity, or even for organizing the freelancers themselves, companies are also working with more business-to-business partners to take advantage of those partners' expertise, scale, and networks. Perhaps in a short time, our typical company design will resemble something more like this:

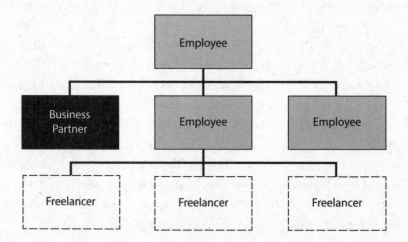

I would even suggest a more provocative image. When I've shared this idea of the twenty-first century organizational design at conferences, I asked the audience to consider a world where many companies are composed of just a dozen or so executives and hundreds of freelance project directors and contractors under them—the gig economy writ large. As I look into the room, invariably the Baby Boomers and older Gen Xs appear ashen-faced and horrified, while the Gen Ys are beaming with optimism at this possible future.

In considering this future, employers have three possible responses to the inconstant tides of their younger workforce:

1. Fight it and do everything in one's power, spend whatever money is necessary, to keep talent.
2. Embrace it and create the twenty-first century community of (mostly) freelancers.
3. Select a hybrid path, distinguishing between talent that the company must keep at all costs and the employees who the company is prepared to let go, because either their knowledge or expertise is replicable or their functions may be completed more efficiently by contractors or business partners.

The first path has been tried for decades and is problematic in that an organization has to ask itself if it really should fight tooth and nail to keep employees who are deeply unengaged. Might those employees possibly do better work for the company from the position of the self-employed, the master of their time and fate?

With the second path, we take apart the organization as we have known it. Employees and leaders emerge, fall away, convene, and depart in a much more fluid dynamic. At first glance, this option could appear impossible or terrifying. But there is a persuasive cadre of management innovators in both academia and increasingly in practice that suggests this model is only the next evolutionary adaptation to organizational structure. Here's Jules Goddard, a Fellow at London Business School and the first doctoral student from that institution—so *not* a Gen Y but a seasoned veteran of both the practitioner and research worlds—making one of his usually delightful provocations:

> In a wealthy society replete with opportunity, there are possibly few sadder sights than a well-educated fifty-year-old still in employment, still reporting to a boss, still working a five-day week, still fearful of stepping out of line and still dependent on the will of others. In today's economy, the main aim of employment should be to serve as a training ground in self-reliance, self-responsibility and self-employment. By the age of forty, no employee should have any further need of employment. Rather, in the way that parents bring up their children to grow out of childhood and to become self-reliant adults, so employment should develop employees to escape a life of deference and dependency and start exercising a sense of their own agency. Yet countless individuals find themselves in organizations where they are led and where they expect to be led. It is a form of learned helplessness.[5]

Goddard asks if there is an alternative: "Might there be another model of collective work that can dispense with leaders and followers and put in its place a different dynamic? What could this be? Perhaps we should look for forms of collective activity that have no need of hierarchy but are nevertheless much more effective for being collaborative pursuits."[6]

As I say, Jules is a wonderfully deliberate provocateur, but he does rightfully urge us to question the assumption that employment is always the best state for an individual, particularly in many Western societies that, for at least two centuries, have celebrated independence and agency. There are undoubtedly *some* organizations and social structures that could do with a little more engagement by choice and a little less adhesion by tradition.

The third path may not be entirely clear as to how an organization would embark upon it and what the trade-offs might be. One Silicon Valley start-up found itself on this path after working up a steep learning curve.

TO EMPLOY OR NOT TO EMPLOY:
THE PATHSOLUTIONS STORY

Tim Titus is the founder and chief technology officer of PathSolutions, a provider of network performance monitoring software.[7] For neophytes like you and me, this means that his software can tell you why your network is slow or what caused it to glitch. Before founding PathSolutions, Tim worked for twenty-five years managing networks for California Bay Area companies both small and large. During this time, he discovered that nobody made it easy to answer the "network slowness" problem. Instead of getting frustrated, he decided to start a company to make it easier to solve this issue.

As Tim hired more people to accommodate the needs of a growing company, he learned about some modern problems with talent acquisition and management. It was his experience with his marketing directors that forced him to question if a full-time employee was always the best solution to create capacity. Tim quickly discovered the truth behind the cliché: "Fifty percent of all marketing money is wasted. The problem is that you don't know which 50 percent!" He recounted, "The marketing people we hired followed the pattern of their last company: 'Just give me a pile of money. I'll spend it and see what results we get.'" This problem illustrates the classic difference between a start-up and an industry incumbent, and why the former can often disrupt the latter. The start-up owns nowhere near the resources of the behemoth but may possess a wealth of resourcefulness.

The giant category kings of Silicon Valley overspend on talent. Unemployment among local college-degree holders is only 2–3 percent. Most cannot possibly be fully tasked, and Titus estimates that "only 20 percent of employee time is spent doing useful work." So companies glutted with cash hire talent both to starve their competitors and to buy capability to solve customer problems they don't yet know they have. In the industry and at its most extreme, this state of affairs gave rise in about 2010 to a new term, "acqui-hiring,"[8] or giant companies' buying their smaller rivals in order to acquire the employees, not necessarily their products or intellectual property.

Tim didn't possess a Midas's treasure trove to employ this strategy, but he could try playing a different game. Losing money and time with inefficient and ineffectual marketing managers, Tim decided he had nothing to lose by importing the expertise differently. Tim asked his colleagues, "Why do we need to hire a marketing director? Let's get a pile of experts, all contractors. We can bring them in as needed. We'll quickly learn who the high and low performers are and work more with the good ones."

Titus also freed his organization to choose professionals based on whether a given need was for a generalist or a specialist. Tim's logic: "As a small company hiring a full-time employee, you typically want a jack-of-all-trades, someone who has a little bit of experience with creating ads, graphic design, messaging, and marketing and communications channels. In hiring contractors, you can hire the 'master' of each category and pay for a portion of his or her attention. This allows you to allocate costs to different activities assigned to different people." In this manner, the return-on-investment analysis of each activity also serves as a report card of each professional. Over a short time, Tim could increase his return by doubling down on the most productive marketers.

In addition to making contracting decisions, considering whether a generalist or specialist is required, Titus also distinguished between choosing to hire or contract based on whether the activity was a basic business hygiene factor or an activity that elevates a company to be different or even to achieve the lofty title of "unique." He recalled the distinction in strategy literature between Core, the few activities that a company does to create true differentiation, and Context, or everything else that a company does just to stay in business.[9] Tim was very clear in his mind that "writing software is our Core competency, so we would never outsource that. Sales and marketing are external to our Core (therefore, they're Context activities) so can be outsourced." It's common sense that Tim would not want to bring in a contractor to develop intellectual property (IP), be it a product or process intended to be a competitive differentiator for PathSolutions, only for that contractor to then sell that IP or know-how to the next bidder.

As he refined this approach, Tim realized that he also had to spend a little bit more of his own time on managing the marketing function. In sending contracts out to tender, Titus understandably needed carefully to frame and scope the problems to be solved so he'd receive the best responses possible. He concluded that, on the one hand, he needed to invest more time in this activity, but on the other hand, Tim developed a better strategic understanding of his marketing needs, which shook him from the laziness that too many organizations face. To wit, abrogating responsibility to a marketing manager means that a company's executives may allow themselves (wrongly) to ignore this function.

Looking back, Titus is convinced that his approach, encouraging higher job mobility, is a win-win for both employer and employee. He explained:

> With everyone's first job, you're told what to do and how to do it. When you leave and join the next company, magic happens and you learn what you were doing wrong in your previous job. In other words, you learn the most when you change jobs because the new job removes the blinders. For the employer, you inject "best practice" only when you bring in new talent and [even better] from different industries. So if you want to learn different and best practice all the time, it shouldn't always be through hiring, but through a rolling, ongoing engagement with contractors. In doing so, you can refine and even redefine best practice in a matter of weeks instead of years. Additionally, when one contractor learned a new "best practice" from one company, it could immediately be applied to my company.

The PathSolutions talent model is predicated on importing as much diverse thinking, coaching, mentoring, and consulting as possible. The model also assumes that some functions, such as managing a marketing initiative or optimizing a sales process, may be organized by projects instead of by full-time employee teams.

Work that is organized more around projects and freelance experts would be taking advantage of a rising tide. For most organizations, the volume and strategic importance of projects is growing. About a fifth of the world's economic activity per year—$12 trillion—is now organized around projects. Over the next decade, organizations are expected to experience a 68 percent increase in project work.[10] Enterprises may choose to organize themselves differently, therefore, to be able to deliver more and more complex projects and initiatives in this dynamic, volatile, and complex operating environment. Companies need a new playbook to seize opportunities faster, an adaptive approach to talent and the skill sets that one might need at any point in time. In just a few short years, organizing company structure around project work, then, may be a much more commonsensical approach than it is today.

FINDING GREAT PEOPLE IN THE FIRST PLACE

For those companies wishing to attract full-time employees for their critical functions such as strategy, intellectual property development, and senior client relationships, we may ask, "How do we attract great Gen Ys in the first place?" My interviews with high-potential Yers from around the world, and my own experience recruiting, indicate that there are just a few promises to emphasize in order to pique Gen Y interest.

The Recruitment Process Will Be Fast

Some of our most celebrated companies—Goldman Sachs is perhaps the poster child here—pride themselves on how voluminous (and endless) their assessment and interview procedures are.[11] In contrast, one global accountancy firm promises that it will run interviews and case studies with recruits as and when convenient, even if that means in a bar in the evening, and candidates will receive a decision the next day! Let me make sure we understand one another: I don't mean that candidates will receive a decision the next day as to whether or not they are through to the next round. By the next morning, they will be told either that they are out of contention or they will receive an offer. The firm believes that its speed and responsiveness was responsible for a shift from usually hiring its third-choice candidate to landing typically its first-choice recruit.

The Recruitment Process Will Be Fun

Certainly, holding an interview or case study over a cocktail in a bar also indicates a commitment to making work fun. Other companies have stood out from the pack with other symbols and indications that working with them could be exciting and entertaining. Comcast NBCUniversal took such an approach at the usually soulless graduate recruitment fairs. Their former senior manager of talent brand and attraction, Kristin Dudley, a Gen Y herself, explains:

> When we were at the South by Southwest festival in Austin, Texas, to recruit top talent, we did away with the company booth and built a yoga and massage studio. We were trying to communicate that wellness could be accessible and integrated into one's workday rather than either-or. It was a huge hit! We also realized that not all the talent we wanted to reach was wandering around the career fair but was exploring the wider festival and neighborhood. So, we went out into the streets, found the popular taco trucks, for example, and ensured our recruiters were immersed in the action.

Rather than opening a conversation about the nature of the work, Kristin started with the criterion of lifestyle and invited graduates to reflect on how they would sacrifice less of their lifestyle if they worked for Comcast.[12]

Certainly, Gen Y is looking for companies where the circles of work and fun overlap. As a high-flier Gen Y manager at a global bank remarked to me: "We're not willing to stick with something if we don't enjoy it. We want to have a go and are always reflecting on our job satisfaction. [Unlike previous generations,] we are not willing to 'grind it out' year after year for some distant, deferred gratification." That insight leads us to our next criterion in attracting Gen Y to your organization:

The Recruitment Process Will Be Cocreated

Dudley emphasized that, at the graduate recruitment fair, she did not bring job descriptions. She wished to communicate that Comcast people have room to define their roles. More companies are rejecting the principle and practice that highly defined job descriptions are the way forward. Such regimented role definition may have worked in some eras and industries, such as manufacturing, where uniformity is key. Henry Ford, a scion of the Industrial Revolution, once quipped, "Why is it every time I hire a pair of hands, they come with a brain attached?"[13] By contrast, the twenty-first-century company appeals to its recruits with the attractive promise, "We'll give you the direction of travel, the goal, and we want you to figure out how to achieve that."

A perfect example of this Gen Y paradigm of cocreating one's job comes from IDEO, the genius design consultancy with offices around the world. Director Sally Spinks explains how the company presents the concept to its people: "Here's where we're going. I'm not going to tell you how to get there. In fact, that will be different for each office based on the market and the passions of the team."[14] IDEO believes there is power in allowing its colleagues the space to own and develop their identities. In terms of how IDEO has imprinted upon its people, the company thinks of its influence more like giving a tattoo rather than trying to create clones. Allowing such job crafting might seem counterintuitive toward productivity, but some of our most celebrated companies today demonstrate that this level of trust in one's people is most often rewarded.

INSIGHTS TO ACTIONS
One Thing You Can Do Monday Morning

On a stack of sticky notes, write down all the activities that your organization does, whether your customers see these activities or not. Write only one activity on each sticky note. Take longer to finish this task than you might anticipate. If you stop as soon as you draw a blank, there are probably dozens of activities that you haven't yet remembered. I liken this type of brainstorming activity to a marathon. At some point, you "hit the wall" and you have to push through and force yourself to keep writing. Imagine the faces of specific colleagues that you both see and don't see on a daily basis. Picture them at work and recall what they're doing. What are their duties on a daily, monthly, or annual basis? There are so many activities that one person in a company, except perhaps in a tiny start-up, would not regularly witness. As a result, if possible, it's ideal to create this comprehensive list in a cross-functional team exercise so you can leverage collective memory.

Now, take two large pieces of paper, perhaps butcher paper or flip-chart pages. Across the top of one page, write the heading "Unique, Different, or Special" and on the other "Fundamental." Put all the sticky notes containing actions that give your company a competitive advantage under the first column. Be rigorous about what makes the cut for this category. Is this activity something only your company does or can do? Do customers *recognize* this and make purchasing decisions accordingly? Or if customers do not have sight of this activity, to your knowledge, does this process contribute to value creation that is unique or at least rare in your industry? Put all other sticky notes under the other heading for those activities that are "fundamental" to your business's ability to run but do not contribute to creating competitive advantage.

These two columns that you have created are very useful characterizations for your human resources department to determine whether to hire a full-time employee, *certainly* in the case of the first column, or *possibly* to utilize contractors to complete the activities in the case of the second column. The reason I emphasize the qualifier "possibly" is that it might still be more economical to hire a full-time employee to accomplish tasks in the "Fundamental" column, particularly if the activity is ongoing rather than start-and-stop or project based. If it's appropriate, share your columns and discuss with your human resource colleagues. It may just change a paradigm or two in your organization about how it acquires capabilities and under what terms.

WHAT GENERATION Y WANTS FROM WORK

Your work is going to fill a large part of your life, and the only
way to be truly satisfied is to do what you believe is great work.
And the only way to do great work is to love what you do.
—STEVE JOBS[1]

When the primary factor in choosing an employer was salary, banks had their pick of top talent from the best universities and business schools, and many freshly minted MBAs wished to make their way into this industry. No longer.[2] Between 2007 and 2013, the percent of MBAs who entered banking from both Harvard and London Business Schools dropped 39 percent and plummeted 47 percent at the University of Chicago's Booth School of Business.

I personally witnessed this shift as I began my MBA studies at London Business School in 2002. During my orientation week, the Career Services representative presented all the statistics that spoke to the School's success in placing its graduates into premier finance and consulting firms. She then, almost as a throwaway, suggested that, "We cover industry roles, too," and asked my class of three hundred new students to raise their hands if they were interested in these nontraditional post-MBA roles. Hands went up across almost half the room. The presenter stared out at us, clearly stunned, and exclaimed, only half-jokingly, "Well, looks as if we'll need to hire more colleagues 'from industry.'" The early noughties may have been the cusp of a shift in career aspirations for many high potentials.

It used to be easy for employers to hit the right notes at graduate recruitment fairs: good pension, competitive salary, clear career progression. Consultancies and banks enjoyed abundant resources, flashy *and* respectable marketing materials to reel in top talent. Granted, the consulting partnership model is "up or out," which implies a lot of "up" followed by sudden and frequent "out." But the social contract was that, if you worked hard and generated revenue, you would become a partner, a colleague for life, a profit-sharing wealth generator. That was the desired goal, and people were willing to work hard for that, so much so that "putting in a full day's work" reached ever more macho, ever more depressing levels of graft.

As the evidence indicates from our survey in chapter 1, though, if employer engagement today is less about money, it's much more about work-life balance, personal and professional development, and organizational culture. Let's explore these three themes one by one.

WORK-LIFE BALANCE

Starting with work-life balance as the factor that is most important, according to the Gen Ys that I surveyed and interviewed, seeking such balance does not have to do with Generation Y somehow being lazier. It has everything to do with the severe transformation in the conditions of employment, when work starts and stops, since Gen Y's predecessors entered the workforce. Technology opened us to the world and opened employees to twenty-four hours a day of accessibility, where never switching off has become the mark of so-called professionalism.

Never switching off has led to all sorts of new ailments and conditions that doctors and psychologists rarely considered years ago. Richard Jolly[3] named one of the most widespread and pernicious of these diseases "hurry sickness." How can you tell if you've caught it? If you answer "yes" to any one of these questions, pause and reflect on thy life!

- ▶ When you put a meal in the microwave for a minute or two, do you immediately have to do something else, multitask, while the food's warming?
- ▶ When you enter an elevator, do you not only push the button for the floor you want, but you have to push the "close doors" button?
- ▶ When you reach a pedestrian crosswalk, do you push the button to change the light multiple times? By the way, I've been informed by city workers who know about these devices that, after the first push, additional taps to the button make no difference. In some cities, even pushing the button once makes no difference; it's a placebo—a device to keep you entertained while you wait. For example, in New York City, only about 10 percent of the one thousand crosswalk buttons actually function.[4]

In addition to hurry sickness, psychiatrists have identified a new phobia plaguing more than half the world, a genuine psychological malady that causes physiological symptoms akin to our familiar sources of terror like spiders and heights. It's called nomophobia, and 66 percent of American adults suffer from it.[5] It's the fear of being without phone or Wi-Fi signal; the term is shorthand for no-mobile-phobia. So, yes, we're always connected, but we never switch off. To what extent? Here are three frightening statistics:

- ▶ Sixty-five percent of Americans sleep with or next to their smartphones.

► Thirty-four percent *admit* (so it *has* to be higher in reality, yes?) to answering their cell phone during "intimacy with their partner."

► Twenty percent would rather go without shoes for a week than take a break from their phone.[6]

You probably buy the ubiquity of nomophobia intuitively, but to cross-check the validity of the issue, an interesting survey asked people to complete the statement, "I cannot imagine life without _____." Think about what the majority of the population would have answered fifty years ago, and then consider what they would answer today. The survey results confirm the worst scenario: "my mobile/cell phone" was the most frequent answer, even higher than "my partner or spouse."[7] A 2011 Google study even shows that 43 percent of smartphone users would rather give up beer than their mobiles![8]

In a world where a couple lying in bed together may even chat with each other on their devices instead of using their mouths, we still seek connection and intimacy, but we default to a new norm for how we do so. With so much communication exchanged through digital media, we can and do work not just anywhere, anytime, but everywhere, all the time. The regular and regulated forty-hour workweek is all but extinct in most sectors and geographies, save perhaps in union-governed manufacturing functions and some government roles.

The influential professor and author Charles Handy identified that the standard measure of work time across a career used to follow the ratio of: 37 x 37 x 37 = 50k, but has now evolved into: 60 x 50 x 17 = 50k.[9] The first equation tells us that, in a previously common career, one worked a total of fifty thousand hours by putting in thirty-seven hours per week times thirty-seven weeks per year[10] times thirty-seven years. Of course, today, that's a statistical fiction. The last time I heard a student say, "No one's working three thirty-sevens anymore," another replied, "Yes, they are. It's called France." It's actually France on a busy week, if you want to get technical.

However, most of us will work fifty-thousand-hour employment careers like the second equation: 60 x 50 x 17, which is sixty hours per week (probably not bad these days), times fifty weeks per year times seventeen years. I know you have about two to five weeks' holiday depending on the country in which you live, but even when you're on the beach, you've still got the dreadful mobile phone that you probably, unfortunately, haven't turned off. And the only question is, "How long are you going to live this nightmare?" Well, the answer is about seventeen years. That seventeen years typically takes place between the ages of about twenty-eight and forty-five, by which time you've either made it or you haven't. Your doctor is telling you this pace is no longer sustainable in your midlife, so either you rethink how to accomplish your job, and you discover some additional balance and relaxation in your life, or you change careers or functions into something more livable. Or you keep going at the same furious speed, sprinting right into an early grave. Some of you are just doing the arithmetic now, and you're thinking, "OMG, my career is already over!"[11]

While it's extremely difficult to remove twenty-four-hour access to work, every organization can engineer balance and flexibility into the fabric of its work life. Here are three simple suggestions:

First, and as I wrote earlier, do not confuse the request for "work-life balance" as asking to work less. It's more often about flexibility in where one works. The working-from-home tide is already unquestionably rising. It is estimated that more than half of American employees work from home at least part of the time.[12] As Sara Sutton Fell, CEO of FlexJobs, clarifies, remote work is not all or nothing: "People might visit clients two days a week, thus technically working remotely, even if they're not at home. Then they work in the office another day or two and a day from home or a coffee shop."[13] I appreciate that, while working from home all the time can reduce cohesion and alignment in a team, surely some freedom is healthier for employees and therefore for the employer in so many ways including fewer sick days, higher morale, and less burnout.

Second, and as we will explore in chapter 7, team dynamics may actually improve in certain tasks, such as brainstorming, if the team meets virtually versus face-to-face. In this manner, harmful team dynamics such as dominance by one personality are disintermediated by asynchronous, virtual discussion.

Third, in a world where Gen Ys seek multiple projects and multitasking, the various teams to which they belong may be located in different offices or even countries. Let the teams decide where and how they meet and interact. So long as they know their goals and key performance indicators, then the leaders would only lose credibility to interfere in telling their teams how to achieve those objectives.

NURTURING THE WHOLE PERSON AT SUNTORY

Suntory is a Japanese brewing and distilling company, founded in 1899 by entrepreneur Shinjiro Torii, who wanted to make and sell wine to the Japanese market. Since then, Suntory has expanded into whisky, beer, juices, canned coffee and tea, and energy and health drinks. Its distribution venture includes large-scale partnerships including delivering Pepsi products throughout the southeast United States. One of the company's whiskies, Yamazaki, is so desirable and rare (after all, it takes twelve years to produce the single malt) that even employee purchases in Japan are rationed. Movie buffs may recall the 2002 film *Lost in Translation* starring Bill Murray, Scarlett Johansson . . . and Suntory whisky: "For relaxing times, make it Suntory time." In 2014, the company acquired the iconic Kentucky bourbon brand Jim Beam for a cool $16 billion, after which Jim Beam's Global Spirits subsidiary became Beam Suntory. Despite the acquisition, Sue Gannon, deputy chief operating officer for Global Development and Diversity, still describes the Beam Suntory company as "a two-hundred-year-old start-up" for many employees.[14] The parent organization Suntory has always placed a premium on entrepreneurship and innovation. Its motto is "*Yatte minahare*," the best translation of which is "Go for it!"—a cultural value shared by Beam and many of Suntory's other acquisitions.

This entrepreneurial spirit can also be a double-edged sword when it comes to holding onto one's people. Sue's colleague Sarah Langley, Suntory Food and Beverage's deputy chief operating officer for Global HR, observes that those Gen Ys who want to leave often do so to join or found entrepreneurial ventures.[15] She wryly comments, "Their ambition sometimes exceeds their capability." But Sarah doesn't think she has to change her Gen Ys' roles, or even promote frequently, in order to retain them. The way to keep them is to offer early, rich, different opportunities, otherwise called the "crucibles of experience" that Warren Bennis identified years ago, which could include cross-functional projects and international placements. As a result, Sarah describes a career path at Suntory as less of a ladder and more of a jungle gym. She even doubles down on this strategy, asking, "Why would you want to follow a linear career path?" Does it optimally serve the employer or employee anymore?

Sarah also observes that high potentials may or may not choose to apply for promotions based on their observation of the quality of life of their current leaders. She explains, "If Gen Ys observe no work-life balance from their senior leaders, and these young managers want a happier life, then they just won't aspire to senior leadership." Langley is quite tactical about each person defining what he or she really wants, though, when asking for "balance." In some cases, if the employee has a new addition to the family, then "balance" might simply mean a generous maternity or paternity leave. For Gen Y, a two-career family is commonplace, so family flexibility around work and personal time is crucial. It might be working one day a week at home or taking a sabbatical.

While Suntory considered tactically how to keep work location and hours to a reasonable expectation, the management consulting firm A. T. Kearney identified that work-life balance also has to do with the freedom to hold onto personal identity, particularly as one becomes a leader and is confronted more with how one is perceived: How do you become known enough to be an effective leader, but maintain a sense of self, keep some intrigue, still have a private life?[16] Work-life balance is also, then, about acknowledging that a leader is still a human leader who requires and must demonstrate empathy, humanity, being oneself and less a facsimile of how a manager in the firm is supposed to act.

We may not ever completely return to the thirty-seven-hour workweek, but we have to consider how to make work life livable in the twenty-first century. Sometimes people look at 60 x 50 x 17 and say, "Oh, that's a huge exaggeration." And, of course, in one sense it is, but most people I speak to are working in organizations where the expected arithmetic is getting worse. In fact, 60 x 50 x 17 probably is not exaggerated enough for many. That creates all sorts of issues in terms of burnout and loyalty. Increasingly, perhaps the discussion with employees has to do less with hours worked or how hard one works and more to do with how employees create value and, in turn, how the company contributes to the employee's development and personal fulfillment.[17]

DEVELOPMENT

We must begin this discussion about employee learning and development by exploding several twentieth-century assumptions:

1. The assumption: Development opportunities are rewards for tenure. For example, every five years, you can go on an executive education course. The reality: Not only will Gen Y not demonstrate this type of patience, but learning is more effective if it happens regularly. In this manner, new or better skills or habits are reinforced through constant practice. Unfortunately, only 52 percent of American workers say they have adequate time for career development activity, and only 50 percent say their employers provide opportunities that meet their needs.[18]

2. The assumption: Learning always happens in a classroom. The reality: We know that oftentimes more impactful development happens both on the job and in

other environments that support learning. For example, if a company wishes to improve its employees' customer orientation, then they might deliver a workshop at a customer site, even including the client in the session, or they might visit retailers and hotels who are world class at customer service.

3. The assumption: Learning is a slog. If you're not feeling the pain, you're not learning. The reality: Contemporary adult learning theory tells us that when participants are in a "field of play," their learning increases faster and is stickier. Of course, intuitively we know, too, that people are more likely to continue to practice new skills and behaviors if doing so renews and reinforces their warm memory of learning those capabilities.

4. The assumption: Learning is a program. The reality: While programmatic learning—for example, a four-day module out of the office—can be extremely effective, it should be supplemented with everyday learning on the job. So many experiences are possible and free that are rich, varied, and meaningful, such as strategic projects, more senior client work, mentoring, reverse mentoring, coaching, regular (versus annual) feedback, international placements, secondments, and shadowing. In short, learning should happen all the time and everywhere.

I want to shatter another assumption that I hear: Learning that diverges from the traditional styles listed above would only realistically work in fun, funky tech start-ups. It begs the question, "Do Gen Ys in major, established institutions have more traditional attitudes toward their learning and development?" I have heard skeptics challenge, "Surely those in the big banks are not that different from their previous generations." But when we look more closely into banking and accounting organizations, what Gen Ys expect from their so-called traditional institutions is anything but traditional anymore. Both new employees and their graduate trainee program managers acknowledge this extraordinary alteration. We perhaps should conclude that no industry is safe from the seismic shocks.

GEN Y LEARNING IN A GLOBAL FINANCIAL SERVICES INSTITUTION

In order to settle the question of whether or not Gen Y attitudes are still more traditional in large incumbent companies, I interviewed the manager for a global bank's graduate commercial scheme and several young employees from around the world who are currently enrolled in this bank's graduate trainee program. At their request, I have anonymized both the institution's name and the names of those who kindly participated in the interviews. I learned that, while the bank's Baby Boomer bigwigs may not wish to dramatically change how they develop their people, their young, hotshot talent has demanded it.

The bank surveyed its graduate talent and asked, "What is important to you?" in relation to the employer-employee social contract. Common responses demonstrated different expectations from their Gen X and Boomer predecessors.

First, the bank cannot expect that trainees will be content to rotate through the scheme for eighteen to twenty-four months, paying their dues and laying down graft in return for interesting work years from now. "This is far too long!" they cry. They seek constant learning and projects with clear completion dates, so they can plan for "what's next."

Second, the graduates expect their employer to learn about them as people, not worker bees, and customize the trainee program so that each individual feels she can fit here. A larger company should imply more, and more varied, possible opportunities: "Find out about my values, what matters to me, how I like to spend time, what I want to do here." Because hierarchy is not necessarily viewed as helpful to these Gen Y employees, they want managers who are curious about them, give feedback constantly, willing to empathize, happy to socialize together, and open to feedback from their direct reports.

Third, they want to be involved in real initiatives, not mock or insignificant projects: "I'm not interested in the formal qualification of finishing the scheme. I'm interested in the experiences I will have here that will lead logically to a bigger project or a more senior activity that will enhance my brand and employability. *Help me stand out from the crowd.* My generation is used to pressure, so we always want to be stretched." Or, as the graduate scheme's manager has observed, "This generation is much more demanding in terms of 'what's next,' and more forceful in demanding that they have a clear path to get there."

Fourth, young talent isn't looking for a job for life, as that would suppress their personal learning and development over time. The expectation is that they *are* going to move on eventually. But maybe, just maybe, they will come back. The institution has made a point of embracing this trend. "It's a good thing to leave and get a different perspective," according to the graduate program manager. "We're seeing that, even though people are leaving earlier than before, some are also returning. The extra places that become vacant also allow us to hire more experienced talent from outside, who bring fresh, new ideas, erode the 'not invented here' mentality that we're sometimes guilty of, and challenge complacency."

This case study illustrates the contemporary, reciprocal recognition by both the bank's novitiates and their managers that the world has moved on from the postwar "pay your dues" mind-set since this approach achieves neither the engagement and retention that the bank seeks nor the respect and development that the graduate trainee anticipates.

This shift away from traditional career journeys has only accelerated as Gen Ys pursue their own personal and professional development at a turbocharged pace. One manner in which this urgency for learning manifests is a greater proclivity to explore more entrepreneurial careers. Graduates have realized that they have the freedom to explore their passions and focus more on their own talents, and the reward can occur faster and on an exponentially larger scale. In seventeen years, you not only can have learned rapidly, you can already retire a millionaire if you hit the start-up jackpot, and you almost certainly will have had more fun along the way. An astonishing 45 percent of MBA graduates from top American universities between 2010 and 2013 started their own businesses directly upon finishing business school.[19] It speaks to the point that human beings are not against taking risks so long as there is sufficient upside. Even thirty years ago, successful entrepreneurs were not conspicuously celebrated. Today, start-up founders can find their photographs in celebrity magazines almost as often as actors and fashion designers.

Gen Y knows that it has more choices outside of banking or consulting, that it's easier than ever to have access to those choices, and that there is less of a trade-off among freedom, learning, and financial reward. To illustrate the proliferating availability of career options, consider how one would go about looking at job vacancies just twenty-five years ago versus today. In 1995, one would most likely look in the jobs section of the newspaper, and that section is already a severely reduced list of all availabilities in the region and very little in the wider country and internationally. Job-seekers would have to scan and edit manually based on their personal criteria. The process was time-consuming, painful, limited in its range of discovery, and required an incredibly proactive approach.

Today, we can create intensely focused job searches in seconds on any number of websites by industry, function, salary range, location, and full- versus part-time versus contract. The ubiquity of LinkedIn means that the high fliers receive inquiries from prospective employers and headhunters on almost a daily basis. So ask yourself: How likely are people today, particularly starting out in their career, going to be patient, pay their dues, wait for the opportunity to do something interesting, when they're seeing new, fascinating roles sent right to their inbox every day? Companies used to have to consider if they were competitive on the employee engagement front about once a year during personnel review season. Today, their engagement strategy and communications are assaulted by their competitors, and by firms they had not even considered as competitors, for their talent on a daily basis.

There is no doubt that attracting and retaining top Gen Ys is ever more challenging, that competitors are emerging from outside one's expected sphere, and that those institutions with the largest salaries on offer don't necessarily win the talent war anymore. So, what are the activities that matter and are worth emphasizing in order to engage our people? One firm over time discovered its own holy trinity: fun, learning, and feedback.

FUN, LEARNING, AND FEEDBACK

There is one global accountancy and audit advisory firm in the top fifteen in the world by revenue that has grown by two-thirds in just ten years. You don't always conflate "accounting firm" and "fun," but that's exactly the cultural transformation that the company found itself embarking upon as its ranks swelled with Generation Ys, who now comprise 80 percent of the firm. The company realized that the majority of its partners would also be Gen Ys in fifteen years. Recruits spent their first four to five years with very clear milestones to achieve higher levels in the firm, but once they became managers, their career progress was more ambiguous and less interesting. The firm's chief learning officer (CLO) and a Gen Y herself painted the problem thusly, "After a few years of progress, you've completed the 'Nintendo levels.' You're then in a 'blah' realm where you can't exactly see the next step, you have to manage others, and you realize that you now have credentials that have enhanced your job mobility including into other industries. There used to be this golden path to the executive suite from Ernst & Young to Arthur Andersen. If anyone in these firms were to go elsewhere, it would still be within a limited set: banking, consulting, audit. Now it's Google!"

So in 2014, a tipping-point year, the company conducted a survey of their Gen Ys, the vast majority of their global employee population. They received 3,500 responses from sixty-five countries, and the answers were remarkably consistent. There were very few times when cultural differences among countries played a role. These young managers reported that their circumstances were almost universally enervating. They were stuck in a no-man's-land where it appeared as if their career progress had stalled, yet their workload had increased considerably. They were also caught in a pincer movement between their line managers and their direct reports, getting hit on both sides. In the entire survey of sixty-five questions, the most damning answer was in response to "Are you happy?" Across the world, the resounding reply was "No."

The good news is that there was a clear, aligned answer to the solution space. When asked, "What are you looking for?" the response was, "Fun, learning, and feedback." The firm listened and developed a comprehensive plan to bring in the fun, tune up the learning, and focus on feedback. Here's what they did:

Fun

First, the working question became, "How can I have a more enjoyable life at work?" The Singapore office volunteered to be the test center for what "a more enjoyable life" might resemble. Singapore sought a very visible signal that they had listened, so they began with the physical office space. They took out most of the cubicles, added bright colors to the palate of the environment, and covered the walls in material that allowed the team to write on it. I should hasten to add that Singapore did not implement every idea just because it was offered. Bad idea: Install a pool on the roof. Good idea: Add a pool *table*, not to mandate that people play pool—if for no other reason, the table would be a prominent symbol of the culture change.

According to the CLO, these simple actions "liberated the creative spirit of the staff and partners alike, *and* improved business performance." Most important, senior managers realized early on that the altered office environment itself was insufficient. The new office space encouraged different behaviors, but it was incumbent on the executives to role model those behaviors so everyone else knew they had permission to follow suit. The office put the final icing on the fun cake with a sparkling celebration of their record year.

Learning

The firm's Gen Ys reported that they preferred their learning "on the job" rather than through formal training. They were not so interested in returning to the classroom as their older colleagues were. The problem that the CLO faced is that it's so easy for development to cease entirely if there's no proactive embedding of learning into the daily rhythm of the office. The partners can say without proof, "Oh, sure, we're learning on the job all the time," and avoid thinking any further about it. So the CLO set out to build a culture where colleagues would share ideas and teach one another as part of their routine. She started by asking in the survey, "Are you innovative?" While 75 percent answered, "Yes," they were challenged, "OK, prove it! What new ideas do you have?" She received nine hundred replies. Through this small step, the firm demonstrated that it would reciprocate if offered the chance to innovate and learn from one another.

The second question explored if the firm was receptive to exploring new ideas once they are raised: "If you share a new idea with your manager, does he/she listen?" Here, there were variances among countries. While 50 percent of the global company answered "Yes" to this question, 75 percent answered positively in Morocco, Thailand, and Japan. On the other hand, the United States responded much lower at 30 percent.

The issue then was how to expose all ideas to the light of day before they are nixed or ignored by the pessimism of a single manager. The Gen Y CLO took a page from social media and suggested "a Tinder for ideas." The Idea Box was born—well, not really a box (far too Baby Boomer), but an intranet site where all ideas were visible to the firm. Everyone could like or unlike as many ideas as they wished, and those colleagues who proposed the top ten most liked ideas would get to pitch their suggestions to the board. These lucky ten were offered a coach and an executive sponsor to help them refine, prepare, and present their ideas. Returning to the goal of building reciprocity, the board committed to invest in three of these ideas every six months. In this manner, a genuine platform was built, on- and offline, to generate, explore, evaluate, and implement innovations regularly. While there are many examples of effective, transformational organizational learning, this isn't a bad one. That this approach can very easily be correlated to initiatives with measured returns on investment was helpful to earn buy-in in an accounting firm.

One simple suggestion was to monetize the firm's vast network. This idea is one manifestation of the suggestion made earlier in chapter 3 of an organizational design of the future, full of business partners and freelancers. At this firm, typical managers spent 20 percent of their time working almost as a placement service for their clients, who were ever asking, "Do you know someone who could do . . ." regarding activities outside the scope of the firm. The suggestion that emerged from the Idea Box was a simple one: Why don't we take a commission on our referrals? It was such a commonsensical, easily implemented idea that the person who suggested it now owns this business activity full-time.

Another suggestion from the Idea Box came from Singapore, asking, "How do we provide accounting services to small- and medium-sized enterprises (SMEs), given that most of that business is going to web services in the Cloud?" When the board approved exploring this question, they did not give money but time—they gave eight Gen Y colleagues permission to take eight Fridays outside the office to work on the problem.[20] The team members created a business plan and found their first client in that allocated time. Impressed and surprised by the quality and creativity of the outputs, the board itself felt it was becoming more open to new ideas, banishing the "not invented here" mentality and exploding the assumption that good ideas only come from the top. The board doubled down on its investment in the SME project and offered that if the team members won just two more clients, they would receive project finance and their activity would become business as usual. The importance of this signal from the board cannot be minimized: It is encouraging proactivity and initiative and also communicating empowerment that Gen Ys crave with business innovations that offer a return on investment. In other words, the model destroys the assumption prevalent in too many companies that to invest resources in learning and development is to make a trade-off against investing in top- or bottom-line improvement.

Feedback

While it is true that Gen Ys seek more and more frequent feedback, colleagues also shared that *when* to give feedback matters. Similarly, the leaders that the firm's people value most are those who know when to take the lead and when to let their teams do so. As audit advisory clients are frequently seeking consulting because they are facing a complex or turbulent environment, the most successful leaders are described as "spikey." In other words, their expression or even imposition of their leadership varies dramatically up and down depending on the situation. At times, senior leaders' long experience is what is required. After all, they usually reached partnership in the firm because they are strong subject matter experts. The really great partners recognize, however, that they have not necessarily been promoted because of great management skills, and so holding back on feedback based on context is sometimes smarter.

It is normal in a firm of experts that people often seek autonomy until those moments when they want to talk through a thorny client or personal challenge. Then they want immediate access to their manager and, if required, quick decisions to follow.[21] For leaders today, the implication is that their success as managers is predicated on comfort with ambiguity, a shifting understanding of what their people need from them on any given day, and the ability to multitask and "multistyle" with direct reports who wish to be managed individually and idiosyncratically.

CULTURE

As our identity with community, formerly held by church and neighborhood, is eroding, companies have an opportunity to create their own authentic sense of community to contribute value and self-realization to their employees beyond mere association with the company brand. This opportunity is particularly timely since we spend more of our waking life at work than ever before. We also saw in chapter 1 that culture is one of the top three reasons that a Gen Y employee will join and remain with an organization.

Some claim that culture cannot be designed, that it just happens. This is nonsense. The simplest and truest definition of culture that I ever heard is "shared behaviors."[22] So if a leadership community wishes the company to display certain behaviors as an expected norm, the leaders only have to agree what those behaviors are and then role model them consistently. When new, young employees join a company, they almost invariably, consciously or unconsciously, look around for those who are successful in that environment and adopt the behaviors that they observe. It stands to reason, then, that if *everyone* in a leadership team role models just a few, specific behaviors, then they are communicating beyond question what it takes to succeed and win there.[23] It's only up to the leadership group to agree what those behaviors are, agree on only a few behaviors that they can both remember and demonstrate all the time, and hold one another to account in not betraying that commitment.

We sometimes forget that human beings are part of nature, too, not apart from it. As social creatures, we flock together. We utilize one another to make sense of our environments. The animal world is no different. Since I learned the term, I've been fascinated with "bellwethers," those animals in a flock or herd that lead the group. I live near a cow pasture on the semirural, verdant banks of the River Thames. I've spent an inordinate amount of time watching those cows in the sunshine. Even though the pasture is enormous, the herd keeps close together for protection, warmth, and to reinforce their instinct for community. Then all of a sudden, one particular cow, not the biggest or most colorful cow, will stroll somewhere else. Without fail, the rest of the herd will follow that bellwether, resettle, and resume their normal routine of eating grass, chewing cud, and staring into space. Not to diminish the intelligence or innovation of the human animal, but we also have bellwethers in our communities whose leads we follow, whether we're cognizant of this or not. We might assume that the most likely bellwethers in our companies are its titular leaders, and this certainly could be the case, though not exclusively. To influence where people are directed, how they behave, what habits they practice, organizations need to identify their bellwethers, convene them, and agree what shared behaviors they will perform consistently and visibly.

I have the privilege of working with numerous clients in many different national and organizational cultural contexts. One theme I hear over and over again is managers complaining that their culture gets in the way of their ability to succeed, win in the marketplace, outrace their competitors, practice agility, or reinvent themselves. Sometimes they tell me that their culture used to be a competitive advantage but now is no longer fit for purpose and therefore hinders their growth. Or they complain that a couple of senior and/or influential figures in the company, sometimes the founders unfortunately, create an overweighted impact on their culture that suits the few individually but holds back the many collectively.

The first important insight to note is that if a team makes some decisions about how it will behave, how it "shows up," then the larger enterprise will notice, even if unconsciously. If the behaviors represent good role modeling for the organization today, then others will start to adopt those behaviors. This is a critical point. Bellwethers may emerge not due to charisma or some magical combination of pheromones but due to their displaying the right aspiration for the community in terms of what is really required from its members. Groups are collectively very intelligent about discerning the right answer, assessing the environment, or knowing, deep down, how to do the right thing. They're not always brilliant at inventing those concepts and socializing them. Therefore, role modeling can create an extraordinarily quick and powerful momentum as it cascades up, down, and across an organization.

It's comforting to note, too, that, even if behaving differently initially seems to be difficult or inauthentic, one can practice one's way into making a new behavior or quality an inherent component of one's character. So, being comfortable with role modeling, no matter one's position in a company, and being fearless about imitating someone that one admires are tremendous qualities.

This concept of "imitating" in order ultimately "to become" is not new. In fact, it's at least 2,300 years old. Aristotle believed that people cannot simply know intuitively or theoretically how to be virtuous; they cannot just study what is virtue. They must actually practice virtuous actions. Where does one begin? Aristotle argues that one becomes virtuous by first imitating another who exemplifies such virtuous characteristics, such as copying the behaviors of a brave person in order to learn bravery, and turning those observed behaviors into habits by performing them every day.[24] In other words, as you practice the virtue you want, even if you're merely imitating another, one day you turn around and discover that you're not just "performing" that virtue, you have integrated it into your being—it's part of you.

A great, contemporary story of this lesson comes from "The Bloggess" and author Jenny Lawson, who writes about her experience recording the audiobook of her memoir. Crippled with anxiety, Jenny knew it was going terribly when the producer called for a much-needed break. Lawson recounts:

> I hid in the bathroom and sent out a frantic text to my friend Neil Gaiman [a brilliant and prolific author and narrator] telling him that I was panicking and was just about to lose the chance to tell my own story. . . . He sent back a single line that has never left me: "*Pretend you're good at it.*" It seemed too simple, but it was all I had, so I scrawled the words on my arm and repeated it as a mantra. I walked back into the studio pretending to be someone who was amazing at reading her own story. I finished an entire paragraph without interruption. Then I looked up, and the producer stared at me and said, "I don't know what you just did, but keep doing it."[25]

Incidentally, the event was powerful for Neil Gaiman as well. *He* then wrote about this Aristotelian episode in his next book, which he applied to an entreaty to be wise: "Someone asked me recently how to do something she thought was going to be difficult . . . and I suggested she pretend that she was someone who could do it. Not pretend to do it, but pretend she was someone who could. . . . She said it helped. So be wise. Because the world needs more wisdom. And if you cannot be wise, pretend to be someone who is wise, and then just behave like they would."[26]

I remember these words in my own career when coaching executives who feel like frauds, and in facilitating what seems initially like impossible culture change in companies.

The first discussion I have with executives who require a cultural change is to distinguish between their culture now, the culture they need, and what simple commitments they may need to make in order to bridge the gap. Ideally, we get the executive team together for this dialogue and workshop it a bit. But before we get to a workshop suggestion that you can facilitate with your team in the Insights to Actions section at the end of the chapter, let's look at an example of cultural transformation from A. T. Kearney, which has been remarkable in that the Gen Ys influenced which behaviors the partners converged upon. It raises the question of who the true bellwethers are in the firm.

LEADERSHIP CULTURE AT A. T. KEARNEY

Stephen Parker, the chief human resources officer at A. T. Kearney, sees that his firm's brand and salaries are no longer enough when competing for the best talent.[27] "Each generation is savvier about the trade-offs involved in just pursuing wealth," he remarks. Stephen observes that younger colleagues consider wealth less in terms of "the great scorecard of life" and more as a means of "offering support for your family and doing the things you want." He is acutely conscious that if his firm is to attract Gen Y top talent, salary will play a bit of a role, but there will be quite a bit more about work-life quality. The firm will need to create a culture of belonging to something meaningful that offers continuous development within the nature of the work.

This last prerequisite for staying competitive includes not only intensive and rapid growth opportunities but also projects that allow people to tackle big business problems while working with the best brains in the firm. The "nature of the work" thus has to include interesting, meaningful assignments, a sense of belonging, and collaborating with smart, creative people.

This shift in leadership culture is also about humility, about every partner asking the question, "What is the value of me as a leader, and what do I need to get better at?" If partners don't communicate an awareness of both the good and the ugly, they come across as inauthentic. To even suggest that one is either omniscient or omnipotent is to lose one's followers. Leaders who take credit instantly lose their followers. "To be smart and a clear communicator are just table stakes," says Parker. "Humanity, humility, and empathy—to manage the tussle in one's head in order to be able to say, 'I don't know' to a client or a direct report, to be open to cocreate solutions with colleagues—are what's required today."

Yes, leaders at A. T. Kearney still need to offer clarity, direction, and priorities, but they can also admit that they might have tough times at home, that they don't always have the answers, that they are, in a word, human. There was a time when embarking on a consultancy career almost meant that the firm's job was to train the analysis into and the humanity out of you by your fourth year. No longer.

While the culture change in the firm is already beginning across Europe and the United States, Parker sees it in the firm's offices in Asia now as well. It is a genuinely global movement, and while partners are changing, one could argue that it is A. T. Kearney's Gen Ys who are nudging the transformation in their leaders. Gen Y analysts and managers want a place at the table sooner, a part in the decision, a voice in the dialogue. Enhancing such dialogue in order to retain the firm's best young talent required changes across every project and client team, soliciting a collective view, and sharing perspectives up and around, not just top-down.

So if we extrapolate what the brand-new Gen Y partners at A. T. Kearney will look like and the culture they will cultivate in their firm, Parker concludes that emotional intelligence will have an ever greater part in internal dialogue, praise for exceptional work won't be an exception, and people will be allowed to focus more on what they're both good at and what brings them joy, which includes a move away from billable hours as the all-encompassing directive. "Our junior people want to change the world, and the firm isn't the only vehicle open to them to do that," he says. "So why can't we allow them to do something pro bono, a project for a charity, or even work part-time for a nonprofit?" In other words, why make them choose one or the other? Isn't such generous use of a little amount of firm time to make a difference only going to earn a several-fold return not only to society but to client and employee loyalty?

While in the past such a description might be perceived as strange or even Pollyanna-ish, A.T. Kearney sees this evolution as critical to its success in an industry whose primary value to clients is rooted in brand and talent. Keeping that talent, earning trust and advocacy, is everything in preserving the firm's ability to compete and win.

The unique A. T. Kearney story reminds us that, while culture is critical to Gen Y, the character of that culture will vary based on context—where the organization needs to go in order to be successful.[28] I don't mean to imply that there is a trade-off between the company's destiny and that of its employees. Surely a culture that works for the latter will only help the former, so long as the enterprise's leaders are watchful for negative cultural characteristics such as complacency and arrogance or focus only on the present (or even worse, on the mess of the past) instead of on the future.

INSIGHTS TO ACTIONS
One Thing You Can Do Monday Morning

Here's an exercise to start a culture change that you can do with your colleagues: Get your team together and facilitate a rich conversation about the culture you have and the culture you need today. Ask your colleagues to think of the people who are role modeling the behaviors the company requires *today* in order to succeed and win in the market. Ask them to describe the behaviors in detail, even telling stories where possible. We're not looking for adjectives like "collaborative" but more concrete descriptions such as "visits their project teams by dropping by each person's desk to get an informal picture of client developments and issues." Write down a sentence on a flip chart for each behavior that has been described.

Now do the exercise again for the behaviors that don't help the organization yet are noticeable and frustrating. Best not to name names for this part. It's not about shaming your colleagues! Keep it objective. Again, write down a sentence for each behavior described.

Ask the team to put no more than two check marks next to the sentences from each list that they believe most help and hurt the company today. Lead a conversation about the consensus top two—the two behaviors from each list that have earned the most check marks. This is a sense check to ensure that the team agrees with this collective assessment.

Finally, have a discussion about what the team, *every* person on the team, can do to role model the top two behaviors from the "positive" list. It's important that these behaviors are within everyone's power to enact, so they must be relatively simple, everyday behaviors. Then discuss how the team can cease any semblance of the top two "negative" behaviors, and how they will hold one another to account if anyone sees those behaviors creeping back in. One suggestion is to use a code word or phrase if someone sees the negative behavior that they can say to their colleague in order to remind the person that we've agreed not to do this anymore. In this manner, it's not emotional or charged. I personally like to use slightly silly, non-sequitur code phrases like, "We agreed not to build otter dens anymore," so that it's really a lighthearted reminder and demonstrates that I'm not scolding but reminding in the spirit of having everyone's best interests at heart.

The guiding principles here are, first, to keep it simple—not too many behaviors to remember or you'll have no hope that anything will change. Second, keep it objective, and ideally lighthearted, so that you can hold one another to account without starting arguments or resentments. Third, recognize that it is concrete, definable behavior that allows you to diagnose and change culture: Agree collectively to do a little bit less of this and a little bit more of that . . . consistently!

5

IT'S ABOUT THE TEAM

Individual commitment to a group effort—that is what makes
a team work, a company work, a society work, a civilization work.
—VINCE LOMBARDI[1]

Another key question from my original Emerging Leaders Program survey asked if participants felt more loyalty to their team or to their organization.[2] The majority, 54 percent, answered that their loyalty lay with the team. While 54 percent cannot be interpreted as a vast majority, it is significant that even this large portion of respondents answered in favor of the team. This turns the classic idea of employer value proposition on its head, indicating that perhaps loyalty lay at a more micro level.

There is a greater responsibility than ever for team leaders and department heads to consciously and proactively develop a team cohesion, a tangible community. Gen Y grew up, after all, with social media, an age of dynamic communities and connections. Institutional influence has less sway over this generation than at any time since perhaps the rebellion against incumbent authority during the 1960s.

A powerful tool for employee engagement is therefore *team* growth. Rather than rewarding just high-potential or high-performing individuals with executive training and professional development, there is possibly more impact to developing the entire team together. Such opportunities could resemble workshops, away days, courses or programs, lunch-and-learn sessions, retreats, among many options. In participating in these experiences, the team builds a common vocabulary, a collective call to action, a stronger culture, and a renewed and sharpened focus. If teams can achieve a profound impact by growing ever more effective and significant in the footprint they make on their world, then their members have dwindling reasons to look elsewhere for career development.

The older segment of Generation Y, those attaining leadership positions in their own right, understand this dynamic better than anyone. As more Gen Ys emerge into leadership, not only will the team value proposition come to the fore of their attention, but the paradigm of community will start to influence the company's priorities: the way it organizes itself internally, creates incentives, and defines success. We are quickly approaching a meridian, and once it is crossed, the fundamental questions of company life that we have answered from the perspective and experience of the twentieth century will be transparently anachronistic.

The increasing value placed on the team over the organization implies a level of independence, even as a full-time employee, for which managers today are not prepared. If Gen Ys largely feel a stronger affiliation for themselves and their colleagues rather than for their companies, then surely there are implications for their leaders. We might assume that for some sexy industries like luxury brands, it would feel different, that the employer brand would create a solidarity and affinity among its employees that the consumer brand does for its hyper-loyal customers. But that is not necessarily the case.

INDEPENDENCE AND LEADERSHIP AT LVMH

Louis Vuitton Moët Hennessy (LVMH) is one of the world's most admired luxury brand companies. You can't go on a real shopping spree on Rodeo Drive in Beverly Hills or through Mayfair in London and not enter a store that LVMH owns. You may buy your briefcase from Berluti, your diamonds from Dior, and your timepiece from TAG Heuer. And how about your champagne from Dom Pérignon, Krug, Moët & Chandon, Ruinart, and Veuve Clicquot? All LVMH brands. LVMH is the luxury brand leader, but Ian Hardie, LVMH's former Group Executive Development and Learning director and now global vice president of Learning and Development for a French beauty retailer, wonders where the future leaders will come from if Gen Ys see the world so differently.[3]

As Hardie diagnoses: "Gen Ys want to make an impact and to be recognized, but do they really want to be the CEO? Coming from the digital habitat, young people who *are* digital like the start-up atmosphere. They'd like to pursue their own interests, their own moon shots. This can be a challenge for established companies like LVMH." Ian speculates that, as a result, leaders may be confused about the purpose of their feedback and how it "lands." Gen Ys certainly expect some feedback and dialogue with their managers, but for them it's more about figuring out how to make progress as a business together, and then how to fulfil the Yers' personal interests, their desire for variety, and opportunity to collaborate in ever-changing combinations with intriguing colleagues. Hardie envisions feedback to Gen Ys as finding balance between two continua. On one axis, you have "direct" and "coach" on opposing ends. On another axis, you have "coordinate" and "collaborate."

As the name implies, a critical internal function of an organization is *to organize* labor and effort. Look in a thesaurus in almost any language for the most common synonym of the verb "to manage," and right at the top you'll find "to control." This suggests that, as a manager in an organization, you cannot help but live on one side of the two spectra, defaulting to "direct" and "coordinate." However, Hardie's point is that, for their Gen Y direct reports, managers may need to create more balance, better understand the context of the situation and the nature of the person to whom they are giving feedback.

A simple two-by-two graph of these two axes illustrates that the adaptable manager may have more options regarding feedback style than we may at first assume:

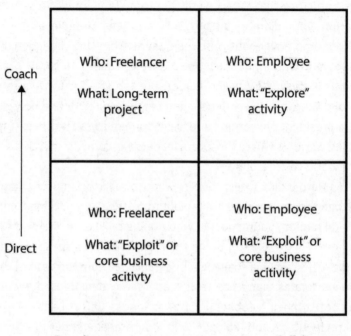

As the PathSolutions story in chapter 3 exhibited, in managing freelance contractors, the manager needs to have scoped the project well. Technical, tactical, day-to-day, or short-term activities require most of all a clear, shared understanding of the outputs. Therefore, the work is more proactively coordinated, and relevant feedback should be direct and unambiguous. With longer-term projects, context or even scope may change over time. So, while clear objective setting (coordination) is still important, there is greater need for the manager to coach his or her colleagues through the changing landscape of the project's life cycle.

With full-time employees, a more collaborative approach is almost always sought, as we have already established that Gen Y rejects the classic command and control management style popularized by Baby Boomer and earlier generations. Direct project and task scoping would facilitate core and/or business support activity (exploit), while coaching would be more appropriate to navigate dynamic, longer-term, strategic projects with more uncertain outcomes (explore).

Many organizations, especially those like LVMH that rely on culti-vating the creative sparks while also monetizing the creatives' out-puts, rely on what has sometimes been referred to as ambidextrous management—simultaneously exploiting one's core business (*not exploiting* one's workforce!) while exploring new frontiers.[4] The ambi-dextrous leader, therefore, also shows up differently to her people depending on which activity she is managing and the nature of the person she is addressing.

As we forecast in chapter 3, the context of leadership, and therefore how to deliver feedback, may depend on whether one's direct report is a freelancer, which is by nature a more transactional relationship, or a direct report, which has other personal development obligations for the leader to consider.

Why should we consciously develop teams if employees feel less affinity for the company today? We have to make our time in the workplace count for more—for personal fulfilment and serving our craving for community. Creating stronger team cohesion, more experiences that matter at those times when the team is colocated, and focusing professional development in teams versus individuals solves the apparent contradiction between the need to strengthen organizational engagement and the need to allow employees to stretch their entrepreneurial muscles and their own sense of professional identity.

INSIGHTS TO ACTIONS
One Thing You Can Do Monday Morning

Whether you are the leader of your team or not, the next time you all meet, volunteer to do a little diagnosis of the group's development needs. This could be as simple as leading a brainstorming session to listing all the strengths and weaknesses of the team today. Write these on a large chart or board. If there is disagreement on these areas, then that's also a good discussion to surface.

Ask everyone to place no more than two checks next to those entries that are, for each person, the team's most important strengths—those characteristics that are vital for the group's effectiveness and for the value the team contributes to the organization and ultimately to its customers. Repeat the exercise, asking everyone to draw no more than two checks next to those weaknesses that most threaten the team's success or what especially holds the group back.

Circle the two most identified strengths and weaknesses. Finally, have a conversation about what the team can do to preserve those strengths. This could include explicit reinforcement of new colleagues' orientation activities, messages, and materials. It might imply creating or reengineering a process, system, or common team activity that would help enable or accelerate practicing those strengths. Moving to the weaknesses, discuss honestly if there are knowledge, system, skill, or capability deficits in the team that contribute to the team's limitations.

If the gap concerns personal knowledge or skill, brainstorm how the team could develop those areas together. For example, a couple of volunteers could study the material and facilitate a series of short workshops for the team so that everyone participates collectively. The team might ask the leader or other senior executive to mentor the team in its regular meetings on the topics in question. If resources allow, an efficient solution may be for the team to bring in an executive education partner to customize a program of development for the intact team, or the group could enroll together in a relevant course. The most important outcome is that action, however imperfect, commences. Even if the learning initiative does not completely hit the mark, asking those tough questions as the team embarks on the learning journey will help to further clarify the nature and extent of the knowledge, skill, or capability gap. That conversation itself assists in alleviating the team's "pain" in that the diagnosis is refined and the solution becomes more targeted.

HOW TO MANAGE GENERATION Y

Section 1 of this book, the first five chapters, confirms that Gen Ys do indeed have different attitudes toward work, how work incorporates with life, the expectations they have of their employer's obligations to them, and what they wish from their leaders. The anxiety and unprecedented pressures that Gen Ys face have led to some responses that managers haven't had to deal with among their twenty-something colleagues before, such as requests for extended leave. At many a conference where I've been speaking, a fretful delegate has approached me to ask, "Should I be worried that a twenty-five-year-old colleague is asking for a sabbatical?" There's no frame of reference for these uncharted waters.

These different paradigms in our youngest people have nothing to do with some kind of biological change—a genetic evolution of humankind toward preferring softball to work on Wednesday afternoons. Nor do they have to do with life stage, whereby all of a sudden our youngest employees will discard their previously dearly held values once they have children and "settle down." We've outlined how the environment in which Gen Y was raised was dramatically different from that of Boomers or Gen X, and that it is how a generation responds to its environment that determines its values and how it chooses to live and labor. Finally, I must repeat my caveat that any conversation about generations takes one into the realm of generalization. It would be unfortunate if one chooses to ignore these trends and how managers and companies may respond, because of the faulty logic that, if we can find an exception, then we can just ignore the whole thing and hope it goes away.

If we agree that these paradigms represent a sea change for the world of business, and how leaders may effectively collaborate with their people, then you might be asking yourself about now, "How should I manage my Gen Y colleagues differently?" This Section 2, the following three chapters, answers this question. One of the very fundamental shifts is that performance management moves from identifying weaknesses and filling those gaps to creating more time and resources for employees to practice their strengths throughout more of their working lives—to find what makes each person great and develop them to be world class at that capability, rather than engineering a homogenous workforce where everyone is a multitasker but is just "average to good" at every skill.

A second shift is that managers must be adept at looking after their teams virtually. This need arises not only because Yers prefer to work anywhere, anytime, and so the ability to manage beyond face-to-face is a principal skill, but ubiquitous technology has allowed and fostered the geographic dispersion of teams in myriad industries in every region of the world.

The third shift, outlined in chapter 8, is a short list of the several new emphases for next-generation managers to develop in order to enhance their own effectiveness, specifically to enhance the responsiveness and engagement of those Gen Ys on their teams. I will introduce the acronym WRAPS in this chapter to keep these simple areas of focus top of mind in your day-to-day managerial life.

Identifying what's important for one's direct reports and responding accordingly would, in and of itself, be a worthwhile investment of time. Empathizing and adapting to Gen Y is also critical since, with every passing day, more of our customer base is composed of Yers. Therefore, implicit in developing the skills to be a better manager to one's Gen Ys is also about enhancing one's relevance for a large and growing segment of the marketplace. In other words, building these skills is also about future-proofing one's business.

Make no mistake, Gen Y customers are researching, selecting, buying, and remaining with or abandoning brands and suppliers differently from their older counterparts. For example, I've worked with several legal and accounting firms that have despaired at a regular occurrence when they've invited a Gen Y client to an expensive dinner or charity event, and the client has accepted, but then doesn't show on the night. The client doesn't seem to value the cost, effort, or opportunity to socialize in the old-school format of "drinks, meet other clients, and make informal commitments" that served these firms so well in the past. Similarly, these organizations tell me that their new, younger clients often find them from internet searches, in the same way in which they might buy a coffee table, rather than the previously commonplace "word of mouth."

In the consumer goods industry, brand owners are discovering, though reacting slowly to, the trend that customers rely on the collective opinion, ranking, or scoring of hundreds or even thousands of anonymous buyers, rather than people they know and trust, such as family and friends. Just twenty years ago, Google was the preferred destination for all searches. Today, Amazon is the first choice for product search. A BloomReach study reported that 55 percent of all online product searches begin on Amazon.[1] Why has Amazon topped Google? It's down to reviews and the recommendations function that facilitates a consumer quickly to converge on not only his individual choice, but that of the wider consumer population. This tendency speaks to the power of crowdsourced preference and how the realm of the web's population is becoming the most reliable indicator of a brand's relevance. We may conclude that being more digitally savvy is not about being "down with the kids" per se, but understanding how and why more of your customers may select your product or service over someone else's. The wisdom and skills in managing Gen Y employees are not terribly different from those essential to winning Gen Y customers.

Hoping that I've convinced you that it's vital to understand and practice how to manage Gen Y, no matter their relation to you or to your enterprise, I'll now embark on a few key themes to do just that.

6

BRINGING OUT THE "BEST" IN BEST SELF

He's overeducated, underemployed, loves plants, is upset about
politics, and lives with his parents: Pretty positive I could write a whole
sitcom reimagining Thoreau as a millennial in contemporary America.
—AUSTIN KLEON, author of *Steal Like an Artist*[1]

There is a quiet revolution occurring, just at the fringes of our
organizations, but this movement is a harbinger of a very different way of considering assessment and development of talent.
Some have called this revolution "positive psychology," others
"best self," some "I'm OK, you're OK," and even "HR love circle."
Skipping lightly away from the pejorative terms, however, let's
just call it "strength-based working." Before delving into this
thinking, let's look at the traditional paradigm.

The ways in which we consider and develop talent are still
largely derived from the post–World War II military influence on
leadership, as imported into the business world when the G.I.
Generation entered the workforce upon their release from service. The dominant paradigm is that our employees are never

good enough, always wary of slipping up, and their fleeting moments of pride and job satisfaction are quickly subsumed by frequent reminders of their own inadequacies.

Consider your own experience of talent assessment reports in the organizations in which you have worked. Ninety-nine percent of you dear readers will recall an almost universal way in which these reports are organized: your strengths and your weaknesses. Now remember how you read and reflected on this assessment. For most of us, it went something like this:

Strengths: *Oh, I'm pleased that I have done well here. I know that I'm good at these things.*

—Reader now dismisses and forgets this section entirely. Similarly, his or her manager opens a development conversation with these strengths for all of five minutes, then never mentions them again.

Weaknesses: *Oh, God, I'm not good enough. I'm a terrible colleague and an embarrassment to my family. I'm wholly inadequate. And who was that bastard who gave me ones across the board in my 360?!*

—Reader obsesses about this section for the next eight months, and his or her manager is similarly obsessed, beginning every conversation with a progress report and feedback on how well the weaknesses are being addressed.

This is a deficits-based approach to talent assessment. It implies that the best way for our people to develop is to focus on and improve those things at which we are terrible. There's a massive and obvious problem with this philosophy. Allow me to explain with a personal story.

When I was about twelve years old, my parents brought me on a holiday to Squaw Valley, a ski resort area on the California-Nevada border that was the site of the 1960 Winter Olympics. Growing up in Silicon Valley,[2] I had no memory of snow and had never skied. I have to admit that I was terrible on skis, just ragingly atrocious. I was holding onto a rope (my only job was quietly to hang onto the rope and do nothing else) that would drag me up the kiddy slope, and I fell over. Since no one behind me could ski either, and I couldn't navigate out of the way, everyone fell on top of me—a novice-skier puppy pile. My nose met my tonsils, as I was squashed into the bottom of a Black Forest Gateau of helmets, scarves, and skis, a tartiflette of flattened bodies and egos. Ski poles may have prodded themselves into limbs and crannies where they had no business prodding. It may come as no surprise that I never clipped a ski onto my foot ever again.

Now, here's the point: Imagine if I spent the rest of my life in a vain attempt to be a world-class professional skier. That was never going to happen, and I don't regret it. I pursued hobbies that I enjoyed and academic topics about which I was either curious or had some natural aptitude. I'm sure that for most people this is completely normal and commonsensical. Yet in most companies today, incredibly, we assess and spend our development resources as if we want to turn our "worst skiers" into "decent competitive skiers." Wouldn't our organizations be stronger and our people more fulfilled and successful if we identified their strongest skills and invested in turning those great attributes into absolutely world-class skills?

The shift we are just beginning to experience is that from deficit-focus (improving one's weaknesses) to strength focus. If we work on our weaknesses, most likely we can at best hope to improve those areas from "weak" to "mediocre" or "barely passable" and only after an unconscionable amount of unfulfilling graft and attention. If we work on our strengths, we have at least some chance, maybe even a reasonable one, to improve those qualities to "world-class," which will have a stronger impact on us individually and on the success of our organizations. I know that I would rather work for a company that seeks to improve exponentially its people's strengths instead of fractionally reduce their weaknesses.

This shift from weakness-based to strength-based assessment will only accelerate as Gen Ys compose the majority of the company population. As one typical way in which a generation develops its attitudes is its reaction to the generation(s) before, Gen Ys are clearly embracing a healthier approach to self-regard, accepting what colleagues can bring to the table, and how we value our colleagues versus the "sort yourself out" mentality of the last sixty years. Positive psychology is also a harbor from the ceaseless economic and sociopolitical breakers crashing into Gen Y's already shaky sense of security and esteem.

BEST SELF AT YALE UNIVERSITY

As an undergraduate at Yale in the early 1990s, I recall that the most popular course was called Psychology and the Law, taught by Professor Peter Salovey, who is now the university's president. There was no lecture theater large enough to fit all 1,050 students in this class; the course had to meet in a campus chapel.[3]

Course popularity is a nice way to see what young adults value in any given year. I know that Professor Salovey is a brilliant teacher, and I recall, too, that the legal spin of his class was a big reason for its record enrollment. It was indicative of the general desire to pursue traditional and successful professions—the majority of my class went on to graduate studies, the most popular options being law and medicine.

Today, Psychology and the Law's title of "most popular course ever" has been unseated by a class titled Psychology and the Good Life, dedicated to the art and science of living happier, with an enrollment of 1,182 students. Even the chapel is not large enough to accommodate the course's population, which has moved to a hall normally reserved for symphonic performances.[4]

The creator of the class, Professor Laurie Santos, speculated that the course has struck a nerve with an undergraduate student body, where fully half its numbers have sought mental health care while at school. Forced to suppress their happiness in their dogged pursuit of getting into a good college, students now have permission to work on ignored skills such as showing gratitude and increasing social connection. Student Alannah Maynez, nineteen years old, explains, "In reality, a lot of us are anxious, stressed, unhappy, numb. The fact that a class like this has such large interest speaks to how tired students are of numbing their emotions—both positive and negative."[5]

Consistent with its preferences toward more varied and rewarding jobs, flexible careers, and the pursuit of the "best self," Gen Y is signaling that we have already reached the end of the line of hyper-competitive, linear careers, where individual happiness and strength-based leadership surrender to hierarchical, "break you down to build you back up" management and culture. Such a macho concept of work cannot continue to grow ever more extreme in its conditions of what is acceptable, but Gen Y has been the first on a large scale to reject this creeping sacrifice of a fulfilling life.

As important, Gen Ys' preference toward positive psychology may just prolong their lives as well. A staggering 40 percent of employees say that their job is "very or extremely stressful." According to psychologist and researcher Barbara Frederickson, positive emotions reduce or even wipe out our bodies' negative responses to stress (hypertension, hormonal imbalance, lower immunity response), implying that companies who activate their employees' best selves might help them to be happier and healthier. Social relationships become more effective, cardiovascular responses to stress are improved, creative problem solving is enhanced, and the ability to perform under pressure increases.[6] Better quality of output, improved work interaction and relations, and fewer sick days are surely a win-win for employers as well as employees.

INSIGHTS TO ACTIONS
One Thing You Can Do Monday Morning

If you manage others, in your next one-to-one, initiate a "best self" conversation. If you do not lead a team, request such a discussion with your boss. But if you are the manager, ask your direct report: "What do you most enjoy about your job? When are you most energized at work? When are you at your best?" Have (what I'm sure will be) a very enjoyable conversation about how your colleague could have more of those moments or experiences as part of her daily work life. The vast majority of the time, such solutions do not require rewriting the person's job description. It's possible but uncommon that the answers you hear concerning when your colleague is happiest or energized have absolutely nothing to do with her job, that she is unremittingly negative about her work experience. If that is the case, however, you might have to delve deeper, a consequence of which may be discussing if this person is in the right role or with the right employer.

However, most of the time, it's usually just a matter of identifying tweaks to help your colleague create a few more opportunities each week when she may authentically experience happiness and fulfilment as part of her job. These opportunities may include:

- ► Seeing a customer or client one additional time per week than the current pattern;
- ► Having lunch in a common area at work more often, even making a "lunch date" with colleagues, to grow a sense of belonging to the community;
- ► Asking a senior colleague to have a mentoring conversation once per month to discuss career progression or development, and when and how to advance that progress;
- ► Taking a course in an area of passion, even if the subject matter isn't transparently obvious in terms of its immediate applicability to one's current role. It might, for example, be helpful in terms of progressing to the next role to which one aspires;
- ► Shadowing an admired colleague or someone who holds a role that is of interest for the future.

VIRTUAL MANAGEMENT IN A VIRTUAL AGE

Whether to extend the talent pool to appeal to a younger workforce or
for sustainability, the term "virtual manager" will have a short shelf life.
All management will be, at least in part, virtual.
—KRISTI HEDGES[1]

While most managers and business educators today agree that
we all need to master the dynamics of successful teamwork,
fewer are convinced of the importance of *virtual* teamwork. First,
many authors and educators assume that the frameworks they
teach are equally valid for virtual teams. And second, many prac-
titioners are still in the experimental phase of using virtual teamwork, so they're hesitant to declare any conclusions on the topic.

However, virtual teamwork will be a critical function in the
twenty-first-century workforce. In fact, most of the Gen Y managers whom I interviewed either currently work in at least one virtual team or anticipate doing so within the next five years. I have
little doubt that mastering virtual teamwork in practical application will be a hallmark of the successful, next-generation leader.

PUTTING "VIRTUAL" TO THE TEST

Even ten years ago, I suspected that managing virtual teams was a critical skill of the twenty-first-century leader. I had hypotheses about how to do this well, but again, I needed data to test these. So while directing the Emerging Leaders Program, I added a simulation to the curriculum both to invite participants to reflect on their effectiveness at virtual teamwork and, for myself, to identify the critical success factors.

I invited participants to complete a competitive challenge, using both face-to-face and virtual methods. Before arriving to the program, I asked students to submit pressing dilemmas that their companies faced. I then identified two of these questions for the students to tackle in the competition; questions were easily comprehended, did not rely on technical or deep, industry-specific knowledge, and would have great impact on the business if these thorny issues were cracked. For example, in one cohort, the dilemmas were related to the news industry:

1. How can an international news division bring to life its new brand tagline, "Never Stop Asking"?
2. How can newspapers make money selling to a Google generation used to reading content for free?

Students were split into two teams that incorporated diverse sets of expertise, nationalities, and industries. They had one week to brainstorm and refine solutions to each question. They were allowed—and encouraged—to take advantage of the "wisdom of crowds" by soliciting input from people outside the program, too.

There was one catch: Team A had to answer question one using only face-to-face communications and question two using solely virtual methods. For Team B, these requirements were reversed. When working virtually, students could use any tools or forums they wished, including video or teleconference, email or social networking sites. We also constructed a simple website that allowed teams to post, categorize, rank, and discuss proposed solutions. The website was also accessible to people outside the course, if they were invited, who could then review and contribute to the online discussion.

At the end of the week, the teams presented their conclusions to a panel that scored the merits of each solution without knowing whether students used face-to-face or virtual methods.[2] After the panel gave its feedback, we discussed what the students found to be the advantages and pitfalls of virtual teamwork, as well as the key differences between working virtually and working face-to-face. This exercise brought to light many dynamics about the nature and requirements of leading and working in a virtual team.

WHAT WORKS, WHAT DOESN'T

Virtual teams that set too many rules or were too rigid about how and when participants contributed were not as successful as those that were more flexible. Different time zones, for instance, required that teams set slightly longer deadlines. Allowing for asynchronous discussion versus requiring real-time "chat" generated higher-quality ideas and responses to colleagues' suggestions.

Virtual teams that collaborated using customized, online team rooms produced final ideas and presentations that the panel scored better than those teams who used social networking sites such as Facebook. These sites often offer little functionality to organize activities effectively, search information, engage in complex discussions, or rank ideas. Teams using Facebook, for instance, either did not participate in brainstorming activities or did so unproductively, perhaps because interactions on the site tend to be largely superficial. Users weren't used to using the site for this exercise's purpose.

Although virtual teamwork isn't necessarily more effective than face-to-face teamwork, we concluded that virtual teamwork that is *well facilitated* and *well supported* by a platform that is more fit for purpose can actually be superior to face-to-face interaction, particularly for large or geographically dispersed teams. We encouraged students returning to work to have conversations with their IT departments about creating customized team rooms rather than relying on existing sites with predetermined features.

A DIFFERENT SET OF SKILLS

The program's participants consistently converged on at least two realizations about virtual teamwork:

First, charisma, a traditional leadership trait, is usually disintermediated in a virtual environment. Therefore, team members could not rely on force of personality, but on clarity and the ability to delegate. "Leading" in these interactions was less about exhibiting authority and more about emphasizing team accountability, reaching consensus, and being open to challenge.

Second, merit has more power than personality or hierarchy in virtual teams. Introverts or those who are working in a second language may actually thrive in a virtual team. We have all experienced how factors such as introversion/extroversion, cultural norms, gender, career level, and reporting lines contribute to only a few voices, sometimes only one voice, dominating.

At its worst, an overly hierarchical dynamic can not only ruin engagement, or even careers, it can aggravate catastrophic decisions. The story of the tragic 2009 crash of Air France flight 447, which killed 228 people, is the cautionary tale. On that flight, the crew came up through both a military and industry culture (though the latter is changing) where the captain is always right, who brooks no "interference" from his subordinates. In turn, the captain's copilots, such as those on that fateful day, do not feel it is their place to disagree with their superior officer whether it is a command, a suggestion, or an opinion.

On May 31, 2009, en route from Rio de Janeiro to Paris, storms lay in the way of the planned flight path, and a rare but not unheard-of mechanical fault occurred when ice crystals at high altitude clogged the airplane's air pressure probes, causing altitude measures to read less accurately. The copilots chose not to alert the captain to the storms that lay ahead, deferring to him to identify the bad weather and plot a course to avoid it, which did not happen. The flight crew made a series of poor decisions and even worse communications that ultimately drove the plane into the Atlantic Ocean.[3] The Air France case illustrates the all-too-common dynamic that occurs in so many offices, factories, and stores around the world, where initiative, productive dialogue, challenge, and imagination are preemptively suppressed.

Most of our organizations' architectures are predicated on a pyramidal hierarchy, which for centuries has suggested the tacit dogma of the manager's infallibility. This canon has ruined many millions of meetings, where idea creation gives way to waiting for the leader to say something, and agreeing or remaining silent, where the extrovert jumps in with a contribution first and often, while the introvert is still processing options and responses.

In a virtual, asynchronous environment, introverts can reflect before answering, the less confident can reply thoughtfully and bravely. Adding anonymity to contributions reduces the senior voices from owning the lion's share of the conversation. The best ideas rise to the top instead of those which happen to be from the most senior. Therefore, if an important objective of any leader is to bring out the best in everyone, then he or she should utilize a virtual forum for at least some discussion and particularly with very diverse teams.

Two important points to remember when considering virtual teamwork:

First, technology does not solve every problem. Virtual teamwork can fail if leaders do not attend to the fundamental problems of coordinating, engaging, and motivating individuals across time zones. It's easy for team members to disengage when they're not face-to-face, so the leader must convey a high degree of enthusiasm and clarity, and agree on who is accountable for what from the start.

Second, assumptions are dangerous. If team members are from different cultures, countries, and time zones, leaders cannot assume that everyone shares the same understanding of how the team will work. For example, will everyone be in one virtual "place" at the same time, or will they contribute on their own time? Our students' most important takeaway is that, to lead a virtual team, they must focus on *team maintenance* (How are we going to work together?) before *task maintenance* (What is the problem we are trying to solve?).

If encouraging a conversation where diverse views are encouraged yields superior outputs, then how and when should a leader leverage a digital forum in order to turbocharge those outputs— to leverage both diversity and volume of ideas?

DISAGREEMENT TO CONVERGENCE: WISDOM IN DIVERSITY

I propose that most leaders believe their teams desire harmony above all, and the most common fear is of conflict. The assumption in this belief is that conflict and effectiveness are mutually exclusive, or perhaps even the cause-and-effect reasoning that harmony contributes to effectiveness. I would argue that the bigger risk, however, is too much homogeneity and agreement. The irony is that the manager seeking harmony could in fact cause his or her team to underperform.

What would a team look and feel like if it sought disagreement before answers, if it did not equate vigorous dialogue with ineffectiveness, if it actively added to the wealth of its diversity at every opportunity? Sounds like a nightmare couched in rhetoric? Not necessarily. Diversity of opinion as well as team composition, if managed well, can build a higher-performing team than the country club atmosphere of the uniform team that most values its homogeneity, harmony, and speed to consensus.

Let us first explore if diversity equals effectiveness. A fascinating psychological study[4] explored whether social similarity helped or hindered a team to be more task-effective. The results showed that, with diverse opinions at play, perception is not reality. Socially similar teams evaluated their own perceived effectiveness as very high, whereas socially dissimilar teams did not judge themselves to be particularly effective. When the teams were assigned a measurable group task, their actual effectiveness at that task was almost the opposite of their self-judgment. The socially dissimilar teams performed their task almost 50 percent better than the socially similar teams.

PERCEIVED EFFECTIVENESS

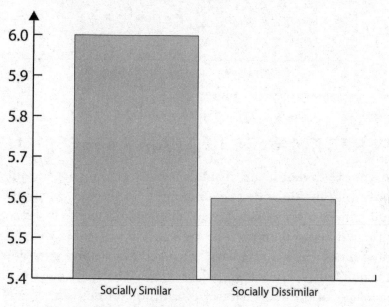

Percieved Effectiveness

Self-Assessed Effectiveness Score

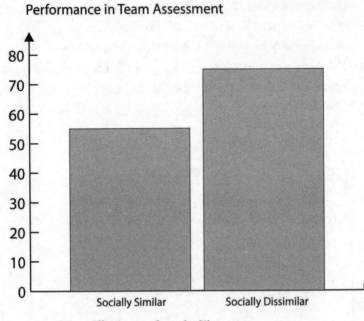

Performance in Team Assessment

Actual Team Effectiveness Score (as %)

PERFORMANCE IN TEAM ASSESSMENT

We must ask that if the dissimilar teams were managed under principles that included celebrating their diversity, would they not only be more effective than homogenous teams, but recognize that key to their success? We may assume that in this situation, those teams would have enhanced morale and motivation to complement their high performance. The challenge for the manager of the socially diverse team, therefore, is to create a norm that listens for disagreement and considers the opposing view rationally with the goal of achieving the best answer as paramount. In other words, teams can be both harmonious and effective if they do not equate disagreement with discord.

When we discuss team harmony above, we may picture a team that works together in the same space. To remove that assumption may reveal further advantages to managing a diverse team that is also virtual. For a decade, a consulting company called How Might operated in the United Kingdom, and it relied on many diverse, and virtual, opinions in order to add value to its clients.

How Might had very few full-time employees. When a client presented a business issue, founder Moti Shahani[5] translated that issue into a compelling question, which may even begin with "How might . . . ," hence the company name. The company then utilized a digital platform to convene a collaboration of experts working toward a solution. Some of these experts presented just a few brief ideas, others more evolved thinking. In this initial iterative stage, the answer was completely open to discussion. Like many social media platforms, members of the network may have disagreed with one another even as the best possible answer evolved and emerged as members added to, "liked," and "unliked" ideas. How Might was predicated on the idea that diversity matters, that the principle of harmony is less effective than the principle of diverse people iterating toward the best solution.

But we all recognize that the world of consulting can be very different from the world of business practice. Would the principle of diversity as a virtue still apply in an industrial context? Here is one example: Best Buy, the international consumer electronics retailer, solicited many diverse opinions to achieve better insight than the so-called experts. Best Buy's vice president of consumer and brand marketing was irked by the criticism he had received that his spend on advertising was not achieving the forecasted revenue. His theory was that the forecasts were too aggressive rather than the advertising not being effective. He set out to conduct an experiment to validate or disprove his hypothesis.[6]

As a controlled experiment, he wanted to see if an average group of Best Buy employees could predict gift card sales more accurately than the financial experts in the organization whose job was to forecast. So he asked several hundred employees to participate in guessing gift card sales for the following month, having only very little historical data. The experts—the professional forecasting team—were historically accurate within 5 percent. A tough test for the amateurs.

The several hundred employees were as diverse as the face of Best Buy itself: stockists, customer service representatives, store managers, and back-office staff. As it happens, their collective, average guess was only 0.5 percent off the actual sales figure. In other words, the employee assessment was ten times more accurate than that of the "experts."

To ensure that this result was not a fluke, this marketing executive conducted another, larger experiment. This time he asked for forecasts of the company's total sales, rather than sales of a single product, over the holiday season. He asked Best Buy's experts, whose job is to make such forecasts, and he also asked hundreds of random employees to make an estimate with a small prize on offer for the most accurate guess. This time, the experts' forecast was off by 7 percent, and the average collective guess of the large, random selection of employees was off by only 0.1 percent—in other words, 99.9 percent accurate!

Now, intuitively, this example may not make sense. An amateur in any field would not typically outperform an expert. The difference lies in the diversity of the large crowd of employees. While no single person would be expected to outperform the professional forecasters, as a group they possess geographically and functionally nuanced information that the experts could not possibly retain and incorporate. For example, the store manager in Minnesota may note that she is having a particularly harsh winter and so will discount her estimate, thinking that there will be fewer shoppers attempting to travel to the store. The manager in Miami may have noticed that the new store is located on a busy shopping street, and so will be more optimistic in his guess. All of those tiny, local adjustments become part of the average estimate. At the same time, those individual forecasts that are widely off are pushed to the radical ends of the bell curve, and so influence the average less than the more widely held view.[7] And there you have it—a concrete argument for leveraging both diverse and collective opinions.

If you're still skeptical, I shall cite an example with which we are probably all familiar—*Who Wants to Be a Millionaire*. This television quiz show has been broadcast all over the world for more than twenty years in dozens of languages while utilizing local hosts. The Indian version of the show became immortalized in director Danny Boyle's award-winning film *Slumdog Millionaire*. What always remains the same in the format across all broadcasters are the famous three lifelines that the contestants can access to help answer questions. The hitch is that a contestant can only use each lifeline but once, and so must choose judiciously when and how to use them.

If you are one of the few who is unfamiliar with the lifelines, here they are:

ASK THE AUDIENCE: Everyone in the audience votes for their preferred of the four possible answers on a keypad, and the contestant sees what percent of the audience has voted for each answer.

50:50: The contestant can reduce the four answers to two remaining possible answers.

PHONE A FRIEND: The contestant may call someone he or she knows and ask for help with the answer.

If you have watched this program even a few times, you would have recognized that most contestants select Ask the Audience the first time they use a lifeline. The average contestant perhaps discounts the general ignorance of the average audience member and so squanders this lifeline on the easiest question with which he or she may only require a little help. Conversely, the contestant typically saves his or her final lifeline for Phone a Friend. It is assumed that this so-called expert will be more effective than a diverse group.

Just like the Best Buy story, the wisdom of the diverse crowd has proven to be more accurate than the single mind by a long margin. If the contestant selects the most popular answer from Ask the Audience, there is an error probability (likelihood of picking the wrong answer) of only 6.2 percent, while Phone a Friend yields an error probability of 46 percent.[8,9]

As an aside, another study has demonstrated with a mathematical model that, if one wishes to maximize the chance of answering all fifteen questions correctly and so achieve the goal of winning the whole prize pot, one should use Phone a Friend at Question Eleven and Ask the Audience at Question Fourteen.[10] Aspiring millionaires, take heed!

I am mindful that the expert on the team must still be given her due. I would argue that the smaller the team, the more this lesson is true. On the other hand, a possibly negative team dynamic that could occur is when the expert is used to being right and may win a debate just through the power of her own confidence and of having more data at hand. With larger teams, I recommend a balance between considering the expert view and leveraging the collective wisdom inherent in diversity and large groups. The following table is a shorthand guide suggesting when and how to utilize the expert or the "crowd" in a given team.

Size of Team	Use of Experts	Use of Diverse Group
Small (seven or fewer people)	Experts likely to provide the best answers.	May not have diversity in a small number so less likely to provide the best answers.
Medium (eight to twenty people)	Solicit their opinions separately from the group to avoid rushing to an answer.	Discuss with the team before bringing the experts back into the dialogue.
Large (twenty-one plus people)	Solicit their opinions; test the average collective view with them.	Survey their views and look for trends and averages.

Size of Team	Use of Experts	Use of Diverse Group
Organization	Gather a group of experts with diverse views to test the emerging views of the wider organization for rigor and/or to ask follow-up questions.	Use social media to collect large samples, votes, and discussion boards to test ideas.

The How Might business model partially uses the technology of social media to remove undue influence of any strong personality. Another solution may be to consider the views of the crowd and the expert separately, so that one view does not influence or anchor the other, and then share for discussion. A final recommendation is to find ways in which the emerging collective view is not a victim of groupthink. The Best Buy example demonstrates how technology prevents this risk.

A diverse group's *mosaic* of different views, some opinions perhaps ignorant or radical, balances the important but maybe narrow view of the expert. The challenge for the manager of such a team is to find incentives and create cultural norms that make the soliciting of views a regular occurrence, while identifying patterns, averages, and trends in those views, as any individual opinion is not likely to be better than that of the expert. Instead of following the cliché of "agreeing to disagree," perhaps embracing multiple and diverse points of view could lead to the stronger though less intuitive paradigm of "disagreement to convergence."

INSIGHTS TO ACTIONS
One Thing You Can Do Monday Morning

Hold a forthcoming team discussion online! If you are not the team leader, suggest it to your line manager. As we suggested earlier, choose your virtual meeting carefully. Many meetings are suited to a virtual environment, while a few are less ideal. Your virtual meetings should ideally be intended to convene on a brainstorming topic, to seek alternative solutions to a sticky problem, or to consider ways in which to seize an exciting opportunity. Neither you nor your colleagues would notice any improvement if the meeting's agenda is for updates or to solve a complicated issue that requires the expertise of only a few of the team's members.

You don't need to have a custom-built platform for this purpose nor any investment, for that matter. Just choose a publicly available, free social media site that enables discussion to be threaded or separated into different topics. Ideally, members can comment on contributions in a fun way, such as through likes and emojis, in addition to adding their own thoughts. Announce and allow the conversation to run for a defined period, such as three days. In this way, you give space for people, particularly those whose thoughts you typically don't hear, to reflect, add, and comment asynchronously. If you really want to disintermediate the overweighted opinions of your senior-most colleagues, ask team members to choose pseudonyms so as to retain anonymity. Take it upon yourself to integrate the conversation at the end of the specified time period, and write a short executive summary at the end of the thread, particularly noting those opinions or suggestions that were the most popular. The next time the team meets in person, you may immediately converge on those ideas and explore in more tactical detail.

8

NEW DEFINITIONS OF DEVELOPMENT

When I have learnt what progress has been made in modern gunnery,
When I know more of tactics than a novice in a nunnery,
In short, when I've a smattering of elemental strategy
You'll say a better major-general has never sat a gee.
—GILBERT AND SULLIVAN, *The Pirates of Penzance*[1]

Paying dues as a function of time is dead. If you're reading this and thinking, "Well, I've been paying my dues for thirty years, and I'm still waiting for my reward," I can only apologize and say that the world has moved on. Executive development is no longer a bonus for years of service, but a requirement to help talent reach their potential when the need arises. This statement implies, too, that, while development may still partially be a recognition, it is based on meritocracy and not time served. Executive development cannot be based on tenure, for example, "We will only give you a development opportunity after you've worked here for ten years." Nor can development be correlated with age, since reinvention of one's career will occur more prevalently. So we cannot assume, for example, that a junior professional development initiative is going to be relevant only for twenty-somethings. An organization will have ever more fifty- and sixty-plus-year-olds who are starting new careers, as longer lives mean more frequent reinvention.

These changing trends and every interview that I conducted with Gen Ys led me to draw at least two conclusions regarding how to think about development. First, organizations must offer many, rather than few and infrequent, development opportunities and as often as feasible. However, as we will explore in this chapter, these initiatives do not have to be expensive. Second, because we will increasingly observe career reinvention at any age, development should not be correlated with age or even stage.[2] A fifty-plus-year-old with many diverse professional and personal experiences under his belt may require different development than a twenty-five-year-old, even if both have the same title in the company.

While we're exploding old beliefs about development, we must also note the good news that some of the most desirable options for Gen Ys today are inexpensive, in fact often free, and represent win-wins for employees and employers. Let's explore these options within a simple "wrap," or specifically with the acronym:

WRAPS
> **W**ork-life balance
> **R**everse mentoring
> **A**lumni network
> **P**rojects
> **S**ide hustles

THE W OF WRAPS: WORK-LIFE BALANCE

Work-life balance is a charged term because there is an interpretation problem, a semantic discord between the generations. After conducting dozens of interviews, and cross-referencing with other findings,[3,4] I have heard the same miscommunication over and over again. When Gen Ys ask for work-life balance, they're typically making a *where* request, asking to work *wherever*, since technology allows them to do so in many industries and functions. They are challenging the fruitless work concept of "face time," where the employee may only leave after the boss does, where they are evaluated based on their visible hours at the mast instead of on the merit of their work. Gen Xs and Boomers often hear "work-life balance" as a *when* request, a desire for fewer hours, a sign of disrespect for their older colleagues, a refusal to pay one's dues. Hence, we don't make progress because we're speaking at cross-purposes.

Does the trend away from face time mean that companies will be less productive or successful? No. The death of face time as a proxy for productivity is long overdue. The horror stories of young graduates and interns napping in the bathroom stalls to cope with exhaustion and eager novitiates illustrating their value by conspicuously working ridiculous hours do need to end. Several studies demonstrate that people suffering from fatigue or sleep deprivation suffer similar physical and mental debilitation as if they were drunk. While I have yet to meet the executive who would be happy to answer "Yes" to the question, "Would you be content if your entire workforce were drunk off their heads all day, every day?" too few approve of a team that judges its work by the value added to the customer instead of by its endurance of the daily slog.

Enforcing face time also harms productivity in the workplace in that it perversely incentivizes employees to slow down, to be less efficient. A number of experiments in the laboratory and in online studies gave research subjects typing tasks that took much less time than the period allotted, but the subjects who finished early had to wait idly until their time expired. As you might expect, once subjects knew this, they intentionally slowed their typing. This is known as the "dead time effect" as opposed to the "deadline effect" where one speeds up as a deadline approaches. If we consider the implications for the office, the dead time effect would imply that workers in a face time culture both slow their labor and hide that fact from their bosses because it's in their interest to do so.[5] They're maximizing their personal return if they have to play the face time game.

While there is plenty of research demonstrating that team effectiveness is partially predicated on spending colocated time together, no research indicates that this must be 100 percent of the time. So, if employees spend a late Wednesday afternoon practicing with their local softball team, they will make up the time later on in the evening or on the weekend. What is the harm if they are producing? Every Gen Yer I interviewed reported that his or her average number of work hours per week exceeded fifty and often much more. If organizations want the quality of those work hours to be as high as possible, then some flexibility in allowing for replenishment and renewal of energy, physical and mental wellness, personal development, leisure, and family cannot but help. As one head of learning and development at a large recruiting company reasoned: "Our [Gen Ys] are as ambitious and committed to their careers as other generations, but they also hold a place for other people in their lives. This affects how they want to work. . . . If we cannot change to cater to them, we will lose more and more talent."[6]

Is there scope for that flexibility to be abused? Yes, of course, but among my interviews of Gen Ys, their managers, and in my own managerial experience, I very rarely encountered an example of someone abusing the system. In fact, I frequently encountered the opposite scenario, that when granted more freedom to work wherever one wishes at least some of the time, most Gen Ys work more hours *and* feel less exploited. Certainly, they have more time in their waking hours for work versus commuting.

Most managers who resist flexible working do so for two reasons. First, inertia: "This is the way we've always worked and organized ourselves." Second, paying dues: "I worked at my desk for umpteen hours a week, never leaving until after the boss did, when I was your age. So should you!"[7] We may conclude, therefore, that the primary obstacle to flexibility is not a complex operational barrier but a cultural one.

Embedding greater work-life balance may also open learning opportunities in that it allows more space for people to choose how and when they will develop themselves. Work-life balance creates the time for development to occur in the first place; it is the foundation from which "development" can manifest in new, personal, and unexpected ways that are fulfilling, energizing, and even idiosyncratic to each colleague in a rich ecosystem of diverse learning that will benefit the company in ways that human resources could not anticipate after even the most thorough strategic planning.

THE R OF WRAPS: REVERSE MENTORING

Author and professor Gary Hamel has identified, "When a company misses the future, the fault invariably lies with a small cadre of seasoned executives who failed to write off their depreciating intellectual capital."[8] In other words, companies can only adapt as quickly as their leaders are personally willing to adapt. I believe we've all observed something having to do with old dogs struggling to learn new tricks? Perhaps a way out of this predicament is for companies to stop assuming that learning only goes one way— down the hierarchy. Senior executives typically have a lot to learn about the changing face of corporate life, what their employees expect of them, and what their customers may want now. Having the humility to allow themselves to be "mentored" by their youngest employees on these themes can yield tremendous advantages, especially accelerating an organization's pace of learning.

To the older, seasoned manager of yesteryear, age represented wisdom because he had "seen it all." Only that's not really true, is it? The fifty-something manager circa 1950 surely "saw it all" but *only in the context of his own company and industry.* Since the twenty-five-year-old employee of 1950 probably planned to stay with that organization for his entire career, his manager really did have a wealth of knowledge to share. The typical fifty-something manager of today has seen it all in the context of one or two companies and industries, but his or her twenty-five-year-old employee may already have experienced four to five organizations and industries in the span of their own short career. There has never been a better time for companies to enact reverse mentoring programs, whereby a young colleague "mentors" an older one—to tap into her own wisdom and perspective, rather than dismiss that rich knowledge because of the age of the source.

What does successful reverse mentoring look like? To begin with, it requires a commitment by both parties. Rank and hierarchy must be abandoned, ignored, and otherwise rejected for the duration of all reverse mentoring conversations, or else the reverse mentor will never be forthright for fear of sabotaging her career. The mentee's promise should explicitly include seeking to understand rather than slipping into "teaching" the mentor or convincing her of the folly of her views. Furthermore, embarking on the reverse mentoring should be recognized by the organization as a voluntary development initiative undertaken *by both* parties, a subscription to their personal growth that enhances their own empathy and neuroplasticity (or learning agility). The strongest mentoring relationships are bilateral: The senior executive mentors the Gen Yer on his or her career or organizational understanding, and the Yer mentors the executive on a range of current issues, such as social media, technology, or even what motivates the newer employee and what his or her life is like.[9]

The young mentor and older mentee should agree on one or more objectives to their conversations up front, such as, "Better understand how social media can attract or repel consumers," or "Figure out how to change the company orientation for new recruits so that the activity reflects what graduates really want from their employer." There should be an agreed number of conversations, after which both parties should assess if the objective(s) has been achieved. If so, why? If not, why not? In so doing, the mentoring pair avoids any misunderstanding or misalignment of what they are setting out to achieve and how.

ZURICH INSURANCE: REVERSE MENTORING THE CONSCIENCE OF THE CORPORATION

The global giant Zurich Insurance Group experienced huge turbulence in its leadership over six months between late 2015 and mid-2016. After the resignation of CEO Martin Senn, who, tragically, passed away soon thereafter, the board selected Mario Greco, the former CEO of Generali, to lead the firm. At face value, this is the story of a venerable institution, founded in 1872, now guided by an experienced "wise man" (a Baby Boomer, in fact). But the deeper story is that Zurich Insurance was about to get a Gen Y makeover at a DNA level—its values—in a very public act of reverse mentoring.[10]

Greco, impressed by his interactions with his Gen Y colleagues from fast-track managers to executive assistants, convened a working group composed *almost entirely* of Gen Ys to provoke, challenge, and reinvent the organization's values. Allow me to emphasize and appreciate how radical this decision was—the CEO of a 150-year-old company of more than 54,000 employees asked a group of the organization's youngest colleagues to create its guiding principles. Greco enlisted the company's future leaders to help make the organization fit for the future today.

This was not a theoretical or intellectual exercise. The shifts that the working group articulated were both significant and salient for how the company needed to prioritize its actions and make decisions for the future. Notice how the values changed from benign, yet relatively unassuming, words (many of which are generic enough not to suggest anything notable to an investor or client) to phrases that suggest actions, and more important, outcomes that employees should work toward.

• • •

From (2017):	To (2018):
▸ Integrity	▸ We are one team and value the diversity and potential of every individual.
▸ Customer Centricity	
	▸ We embrace new ideas to exceed our customers' expectations.
▸ Sustainable Value Creation	
▸ Excellence	▸ We deliver on our promises and stand up for what is right.
▸ Team Spirit	

The difference is a remarkable guiding light that illuminates a path away from corporate-speak: "integrity" and "excellence," anyone? Who could argue with those words? But what do they imply that I'm supposed to do on Monday morning? Would anyone really go to work saying, "Well, I was planning on doing a mediocre job, but then I remembered that I'm supposed to be excellent." Instead, we read a rather clear shift toward significant Gen Y paradigms. These include diversity, specified by the value of the individual and his or her unique perspective rather than hiring to demographic targets, and higher purpose (doing what is right) beyond maximizing shareholder value. Consistent with embracing diverse colleagues and hopefully welcoming their different thinking, the focus on "embracing new ideas" is also a more daring move in an insurance industry that traditionally values conservative, tried-and-true practices and mind-sets, as exemplified in the venerable New York Life Insurance Company's value to "honor the legacy."

It's possible but doubtful that Mario Greco may have reached similar values through dialogue with his executive committee, but the more likely outcome would have reflected the condition that long-standing employees tend to extrapolate the future from the past. The older executives become, and the more their reputations are intertwined with the status quo departments, services, and brands that they grew, the more those leaders are emotionally invested in the past instead of preparing their organizations for the future. Greco's plan, therefore, to deploy his high-potential Gen Ys to the task of value-creating and soul-crafting on behalf of the "Zurich to come" was a phenomenally rare and humble act.

At the same time, those young individuals got so much more in return for the investment of their time and thinking. The values working group had a powerful crucible of experience[11]—an early, rich, and decidedly different experience that developed them personally and professionally, with access to the highest level of their company's leadership, and a once-in-a-lifetime opportunity to pave the path for all their colleagues today and for many years to come.

THE A OF WRAPS:
ALUMNI NETWORK

If employees are most probably not going to work for one organization for their entire careers, how can companies embrace that reality and still create win-wins? We can learn a great deal from many of the most prominent professional service firms, such as McKinsey & Company and Accenture, which cultivate strong alumni communities among their former employees. In doing so, the firms cultivate loyal future clients and increase the possibility that some of their alumni will return to their consulting companies a second or even third time with all the enhanced development, experience, and leadership lessons that these alumni have acquired and without the firms having to pay for these.

If there's a clear advantage for employers, there is certainly also a benefit for their alumni, particularly those who leave to become freelancers. The alumni network from their former company provides community, sometimes even a physical place to which to return. Duke Corporate Education collaborates with about 1,500 freelance educators and executive coaches around the world. Many of them tell me that the association with Duke is especially dear to them because it provides a sense of family and a "home" that they might otherwise lose if their professional interactions only careened transactionally from client to client. As social animals, we seek our tribes for like-minded peers, for different and stimulating thinking and discussion, for role models, for inspiration. Without these networks, the self-employed are at even greater risk of the loneliness epidemic that some researchers report is hitting the workplace.[12]

Selfishly, the continued association with Duke potentially offers a more predictable income for its associates. Even if that is across several clients, it is still through one channel. Playing in the gig economy might then be about finding balance between predictability and possibility, viability (knowing where your next check is coming from) and vitality (feeling authentic in your own brand).[13]

THE P OF WRAPS: PROJECTS

All the Gen Ys I interviewed at some point emphasized that they craved ever more challenging and senior responsibilities. When I asked if that meant that they expected regular promotions, they vigorously replied, "No." When I asked if they meant courses, they said, "Not necessarily." The most common description I heard of a challenging responsibility was a project, which could be any professional experience that stimulated the individual, gave them more senior access to colleagues or customers, a greater influence in decision making, and ideally an activity that helped them "badge" their résumés. When I asked for examples of projects, what struck me most was how simple and inexpensive most of them are:

- ▶ Secondments or temporary roles in other functions, departments, or offices;
- ▶ International placements;
- ▶ Shadowing roles to which the employee aspires;
- ▶ Mentoring by the role models in the organization;
- ▶ Coaching to enhance self-awareness, effectiveness in-role, and readiness for the next position;

▸ More senior client, customer, product, or service development projects.

The manner of these myriad projects allows for development to occur regularly and on the job instead of narrowly defining development as served by infrequent courses or promotions. For a company, offering these "crucibles of experience" requires alignment and communication more than funding. Given the cost of recruiting top talent, the return on such meager investment is impressive if it contributes to attracting and keeping one's stars.

THE S OF WRAPS: SIDE HUSTLES

Remember Kristin Dudley, the Gen Y former employer branding manager for Comcast NBCUniversal? Kristin saw early on that most of her graduate recruits had a "side hustle" going on in addition to their full-time employment: a start-up, a charity, a website, and so on. Call it variety, call it insurance, call it stimulation, call it making an outsized difference in one's life beyond the definition of a job. Growing up in less certain times, watching their parents and older siblings' fortunes crushed in the Great Recession, Gen Ys see their careers more as a series of potential wanderings than linear paths. What better way to have career insurance than to cultivate career options and to nurture them before those options are required, rather than desperate, convulsive, real-time reinvention? Rather than think of these endeavors as distractions, Kristin chose to interpret them as opportunities for professional development and engagement.

In addition, any of these activities may become opportunities for the company itself: entrepreneurial ventures, product prototypes, and social responsibility initiatives. Historically, personal passion projects developed outside of the day job have yielded massive new products for employers, including W. L. Gore's guitar strings, Intuit's SnapTax, and Google's Gmail. Should a company decide to back any of these side hustles, they also create future managerial roles and upside for the people who founded them. For example, Nokia offers grants of up to 25,000 euros plus coaching and mentoring for promising business plans that their employees devise, but Nokia does not take a stake in these businesses.[14] The ultimate purpose of knowingly tolerating, or even nurturing, the side hustle is simply to encourage innovation and agility.

Once a critical mass of employees is pursuing their passions outside of the strict parameters of role definitions, the organization has de facto built adaptability, creativity, and a culture of prototyping into its DNA, as personal initiatives are continuously conceived, fostered, killed, or evolved. However creative you think your colleagues are, if they don't have the chance to pursue something that is not mission critical, most of their creative capacity will go unexploited. If you don't create room for aspiring entrepreneurs inside your organization, they'll simply leave and compete with you from outside. And unfortunately, it's almost a maxim that start-ups disrupt the stalwarts more than the other way around. Why? Start-ups have the hunger and the tolerance to give innovation freer reign.

I hope that you will share and apply WRAPS in your team or organization. My own conversations with those in the business world, both younger and older, have reinforced my confidence that WRAPS is a simple and easily applicable framework to enhance development that works for all parties.

INSIGHTS TO ACTIONS
One Thing You Can Do Monday Morning

If you are a Gen Xer or Baby Boomer, create a reciprocal mentoring relationship with a Gen Y colleague. Start with a contracting discussion about what you both wish to get out of your future conversations. Also, agree on the frequency of your meetings, how many you'll have, and stick to that commitment. The Yer may want advice on learning and development that he can get on the job with different or more challenging experiences. The Xer or Boomer may want to learn more about how the Yer uses social media, whether that creates customer insights that had previously been untapped, or simply how Gen Y views today's leadership community and how the Yer predicts that he might lead, given the opportunity. Where are the differences and the similarities between your perspectives, and how might you narrow the gaps?

What are the implications in terms of how the leaders in the organization might talk about the company in recruitment conversations, structure learning for their younger employees, and motivate and manage this community differently, rather than stubbornly adhere to methods and styles that they experienced "when they were that age" yet don't yield the same result today?

NEXT GENERATION LEADERSHIP

We've navigated the conundrums of how to better manage Gen Ys. If they require a different manner of leadership, then surely as they grow into the founders and managers of our organizations, they will lead differently than our current role models do. It is critical to think ahead as to what this new paradigm of leadership may resemble, so that our companies will be prepared to step into the future rather than to be dragged kicking and screaming. If we ignore the vanguard leadership of tomorrow and succumb to mewling and fretting, consumed from the inside in distracted, vain battles to retrench the mind-sets of yesterday, the competition will inevitably seize the day.

Gen Y already suggests different answers to some of our most acute perturbations. How can we be truly agile? How do we authentically live our collective purpose, and in so doing, help our people connect to their own personal purpose? And would these routes lead to financial success, or are they misguided journeys toward a bewildered and distracted irrelevance?

9

AGILITY—HARD TO TALK ABOUT AND HARDER STILL TO MASTER

Experiment
Make it your motto day and night
Experiment
And it will lead you to the light
—MABEL MERCER, "Experiment"[1]

The greatest teacher, failure is.
—YODA, *Star Wars: The Last Jedi*[2]

One cannot enter a boardroom anywhere in the world without stumbling through another executive entreaty for both the organization and its people to be more agile. As clichéd as "think outside the box" was in the noughties years, "think agile" has been our catchphrase for the teens. There's so much angst out there about being agile—a dream state pursued with the same passionate yet desperate rhetoric of weight loss in January.

While I'm on the topic of clichés, I do think I may stab my own hand with a dull pencil if I hear another conference speaker traipse through a lengthy summary of the term VUCA: Volatility, Uncertainty, Complexity, Ambiguity.[3] It might be just me; I recognize I'm fortunate to be in the executive education space. Indisputably, though, the *rate of change* itself is accelerating exponentially. We're not in a VUCA world anymore; we're in a world where the VUCA has metastasized into a kind of entity from another dimension due to its own frantic pace. A Fortune 500 CEO and chairman lamented that, in the earlier days of his career, forecasting changes in the business environment was akin to "keeping your eyes on the horizon while rocking gently on a swing. Today, it's like trying to watch the horizon while riding a roller coaster."

Of course, technology itself, and specifically easily accessible processing power, explains one of the reasons for acute disruption occurring on a pandemic scale today. Using typical wage rates in the United States, in 1970, the average person would have to work for 1.24 *lifetimes* in order to afford one MIPS (Million Instructions Per Second) of processing power. In 1984, it would have taken fifty-two *hours*. In 1997, it was just twenty-seven *minutes*.[4] Today, the same worker can afford that one MIPS from *one-third of a second* of labor. The scale, speed, and accessibility of processing power imply that digitization and big data together give companies the potential to disrupt their competitors at lightning speed. No longer can any incumbent expect to scan the horizon and accurately identify the next existential threat, no matter how powerful its telescope.

I shouldn't overelaborate in order to convince you that change is the disease of our day to those who tie their fortunes to incremental business improvement (a very desirable and in-demand capability only a few short years ago), and the boon of our age to those willing to test fundamentally, and even blow up, the status quo before the competition does. The prescient Charles Dickens could have easily described our business environment today in one of his finest opening lines: "It was the best of times. It was the worst of times."[5]

We can indeed learn a great deal from our youngest employees about tapping the agile spirit. The manner in which Gen Ys manage their careers is the epitome of agility. From one perspective, the human resources officer laments that she is unable to retain her Gen Y employees. From the other perspective, we could ask ourselves: "What does Gen Y gain by taking low-investment [in time and emotion] job opportunities?" Just for starters, the twenty-something worker today gains a rich diversity of experiences, functions, industries, customers, business, operating, and management models that his or her grandparents never enjoyed. The Baby Boomer paradigm was that you learned "the way things are done around here" and then spent a lifetime mastering *that.* Perhaps but one reason that managers today find Gen Y challenging is that those young neophytes are justifiably challenging the status quo, as they are personally familiar with some of the alternatives.

Here is a short list of some of the most impactful Gen Y–type approaches to how we may work and collaborate in order to weave agility into an organization: intrapreneurship, crowdsourcing, and experimentation.

INTRAPRENEURSHIP

Steve Jobs required the agility of a start-up, freed from the bureaucracy of the larger enterprise, to achieve his ambition to engineer the Apple Macintosh personal computer, so he created a company within the company. He assembled a Mac development team and housed them in a separate building complete with a pirate flag on the roof as a signal that it was most certainly not business as usual.[6] The Mac team members had permission to tear up the rulebook for how Apple usually developed products and created their own processes and ways of working.[7] In effect, the Mac team was enabled to act as if they were a start-up, even though their salaries came from a corporate giant. Then, once his team of internal entrepreneurs had come up with the goods, he harnessed the capability of Apple to scale, market, and distribute to millions of consumers quickly, sparking the next personal computing revolution.

Over the last ten years, I've noticed a broad change in what learning and development companies are asking for in my own professional context of executive education. It used to be about skills—boosting a company's performance by enhancing the input of its key talent. Today, organizations are talking more about their capabilities as a whole and one capability above all—agility. They are asking how they, like Apple, can be both big *and* fast? How can senior executives spot threats and opportunities sooner and respond more quickly? How can they have the mind-set of entrepreneurs when they are in charge of organizations many times larger than start-ups?

The answer involves exploding the decades-old paradigm of the "all-knowing" leader. The world today is just too complex and companies too big for managers, senior executives, and CEOs to know everything about everything. They shouldn't be solely responsible for knowing what's over the horizon or for deciding on the best response to every new threat or opportunity. Instead they need to admit "I don't know what I don't know" and make more use of the company's internal resources. They need to become intrapreneurial, or entrepreneurial from inside a big organization—having an entrepreneurial mind-set and the freedom to act as such without having to break away on one's own.

Being intrapreneurial is about pushing authority down, flattening the hierarchy, and saying that what any individual brings to work can be as powerful and important as what the CEO brings. Take the example of Toyota. For many years, General Motors (GM) knew that its Japanese rival was putting out cars at a faster rate and with fewer manufacturing errors, but GM couldn't figure out how. They returned to the problem again and again—Toyota even allowed them to visit their factories—but for decades GM simply couldn't pinpoint the solution.

Finally it clicked. The senior management at Toyota had devolved responsibility for its production line to the experts—the people actually working on the factory floor. Those on the manufacturing line were best placed to spot any problems in the process or ways to improve. And they were the ones given the authority to bring the whole production line to a halt if need be. At GM, such a potentially expensive decision could only be taken by an executive far removed from the factory floor via a series of lengthy and complicated protocols. What Toyota was doing was so alien that the GM team couldn't diagnose what they were seeing.[8] For decades, the agility of the Japanese giant's decision-making had given it a real competitive advantage.

Aligning jobs, teams, and functions to be more intrapreneurial can imply a number of things. Often, it's about creating small teams with the authority to shape and execute individual projects, just as Steve Jobs did. This kind of responsibility and accountability is exactly what the Generation Y employees in many companies want, and it means that the company as a whole can benefit from the agility and entrepreneurial spirit of its smaller teams.

Being intrapreneurial also means opening up channels of communication so that knowledge is constantly shared throughout the company. Leaders need to be encouraged to canvass opinion from everyone, even from those who have just joined their workforce. What are they seeing? What do they think should be the company's next move or product? With today's communications and media, this kind of information gathering and sharing can be achieved on a much larger scale, so that decisions can be made through a process of crowdsourcing—more on this later in the chapter.

Another way to be intrapreneurial is via the inorganic path— finding start-ups to buy can help the parent company deal with issues more quickly and effectively. It also means allowing those start-ups to continue acting like start-ups even after they have been acquired. Then, when their agility leads them to valuable insights or opportunities, the parent can quickly and profitably scale those up. The philosophy behind this approach is that a large company's core competence is scale, whereas a start-up's is speed and agility. So, rather than trying to be nimble, the corporate behemoth buys the capability. It's a strategy that companies like Cisco and Google do very well.[9] Of course, the trick is in ensuring that the acquirer doesn't kill its acquisition's entrepreneurial spirit by "onboarding" the acquired into its own bureaucracies.

Being intrapreneurial also involves a culture change that bigger companies often struggle with—questioning their structures, systems, values, and incentives—but the results can be transformational, marrying agility to scale and making the most of one's wider resources. It provides a competitive advantage that can last for years.

HAIER'S INIMITABLE CULTURAL ADVANTAGE—MICROENTERPRISES

Haier Group, headquartered in Qingdao, China, is the fastest growing and largest provider of white goods (washer/driers, refrigerators, air and water purifiers, among many others) in the world. In his thirty-five years as CEO, Zhang Ruimin has led Haier through several transformations. The first, in the 1980s, was to differentiate itself through product quality. The second, in the 1990s, was to redefine itself from a manufacturer to a customer solution provider. The third, in the 2000s, was to reorganize the company into self-managed teams. This makeover was cultivated through the philosophical lens that all employees should be as near as possible to the customer. That would never happen in a gigantic, hierarchical organizational structure. Ruimin's solution was to almost completely flatten the company, so there are only three levels between a frontline worker and the CEO. Almost all employees reside in what Zhang calls "microenterprises" or teams that operate like entrepreneurial start-ups, self-governed and organized.[10]

Ruimin is a scholar of management literature. Inspired by the late Peter Drucker's proposition that the purpose of business is not to make money but to meet the needs of customers, and those companies that do the best in this mission will succeed in terms of increased profits, return to shareholders, and income to employees (more on this theme in chapter 11), Ruimin organized Haier to minimize the distance between employee and consumer. Haier's term for this is "*rendanheyi*," which in written form combines the Chinese characters that represent creating value for customers and value received by employees.

Each microenterprise is assembled, through self-selection, around a consumer need. There are three varieties of microenterprises. One is a market-facing unit that is based on Haier's legacy appliance business. Another is an entirely new business such as their Thunderobot e-gaming product. A third is a "node" that sells parts, research and design, manufacturing, enterprise, and human resource support. Unlike many businesses, who rely exclusively on their business partnering support and cannot use alternatives to their internal providers, the nodes compete with any and all external suppliers for their services to Haier's microenterprises. On the one hand, they charge for their internal services, yet on the other hand, their fees are predicated on meeting their service and customer promise.[11]

Individuals apply to a team that appeals to them. Each team can vote an applicant in or out based on the quality of their ideas, their invention, and/or the feasibility of their go-to-market plan. Similarly, team members can be voted out if they're not delivering on their internal promise. Only the team needs to decide when and how it will communicate with consumers. If they discover that a customer need cannot be met profitably, then the team disassembles, and each member seeks a new team. The microenterprise can also elect and de-select its leader; any person in the company can nominate herself to lead a different team if that individual believes that she can do a better job.[12]

The microenterprise is assigned ambitious quality and profit targets. Quality metrics are tracked every day, with bonuses awarded if standards are met. Profit targets are also important because a team can never operate like an entrepreneurial company if it ultimately is not responsible for both the top and bottom line. A pretty good definition of "entrepreneur," after all, is one who identifies and meets a market need and can serve that need profitably. Haier is just applying that same definition to its employee experience and motivation. If profit targets are met, the bonus for the team can be significant, even life-changing. Conversely, the team that doesn't perform will not earn sufficient income to remain as a team for long if it cannot turn their situation around.

All of the above probably sounds great in terms of the attention that the customer receives and the autonomy that the employee enjoys. The obstacle, the possible detractor, is of course the leader within Haier, who perhaps for decades, has hoisted herself, step by excruciating step, up the corporate ladder. In most companies, flattening hierarchy would signify that executives lose their privileges, prerogatives, budgets, and teams. For the last 150 years, the scorecard for career success has been measured on the size of your budget, the number of people under your name in the organizational pyramid, and the floor where your office is located (the higher, the better). Unluckily, it is these same executives who also wield the authority to change this, though such a decision may diminish their power, damage their authority, and injure their self-esteem.

Zhang recognizes the high stakes that are involved in changes of such magnitude: "There will be an earthquake if it is not properly handled." But he also believes it is the only course of action that will allow a large company to succeed in a highly volatile era. The goal of any large company, he says, is to "lose control step by step." In other words, Zhang believes that Haier is like any other major organization in that it will have to learn to maintain its identity, the quality of its products and services, and its customer relationships, while being prepared to give up everything else. Haier's role in this new world is as a pioneer with few role models.[13]

Haier demonstrates the value of getting close to the customer in that the organization can assemble and reassemble itself quickly based on a continuous flow of information and insights from its customers. If receiving and analyzing customer data is one key component to drive agility, then another mechanism can be equally useful in gathering and responding to intelligence—crowdsourcing.

CROWDSOURCING

As just one example of the ridiculous pace of disruptive change today, consider the phenomenon of crowdsourced finance. In 2012, crowdsource funding globally composed only 14 percent of the total financing provided by venture capital. Today, the global sum of all crowdfunding *exceeds* all venture capital by several billion dollars.[14] This is good news for burgeoning entrepreneurs. It's also good news for individual investors in considering where the "smart money" is going. Crowds may not be great at creating exceptional ideas, but they do very well in evaluating and rewarding good ideas quickly. If we only look at financial return, consider all the securities in the New York Stock Exchange (NYSE) as a portfolio of investments, the ultimate example of crowd sentiment. The return on the NYSE has collectively performed far better than most individual companies that are listed *in* the NYSE.[15] While huge groups of investors are sometimes prone to panic, they are quick to seize on enthusiastic sentiment and inject capital at astonishing speed. Luckily, over the long term, the market's optimism has rewarded both investors and ventures far more than pessimism has punished them.

Crowds also mitigate some of the biases of individual investors. For example, venture capitalists have been historically more likely to invest in the business plans of male entrepreneurs versus female.[16] A crowdfunding site with many investors and entrepreneurs allows the ideas of highest merit to attract the greatest volume of finance, similar to the advantages of virtual teamwork that were discussed in chapter 7. The ability of entrepreneurial ventures to achieve escape velocity, the ease of "speed-dating" between angel investors and entrepreneurs, and the deep and broad assessment of ideas through crowdfunding platforms are all energizing a new golden age for entrepreneurship, which should simultaneously turbocharge innovation *and* industry disruption for decades to come.

Aside from crowdfunding and identifying good ideas, crowds can also be world class at solving long-standing problems too difficult for any single mind to crack. Biochemists researching a cure for HIV struggled to determine the molecular structure of an enzyme from an AIDS-like virus found in rhesus monkeys. If they could crack the structure, they could, by extension, conceivably design a drug to stop the virus in humans. Computers failed, too, at solving this puzzle, as it involves spatial reasoning, a skill that is still beyond the capabilities of computational power.

Researchers at the University of Washington turned to the wisdom of the crowd to unravel this puzzle. More specifically, they looked to users of an online collaborative game called Foldit. Foldit asks gamers to rearrange virus-like structures in a manner that would make these molecules behave more efficiently or, more accurately, require less energy: The lower the energy, the higher the player's score. So the game attracts people who love nothing more than to manipulate digital molecules. Now this may not float *your* boat, but there are plenty of players out there who adore it—over a quarter of a million, in fact. While fewer than a dozen of these Foldit gamers took up the university's challenge to unravel the rhesus monkey enzyme, they collectively cracked the conundrum in under ten days. That's agility personified. This is hopefully but the first example of a long-standing scientific problem solved by online, crowdsourced gamification.[17]

EXPERIMENTATION

In essence, the Gen Y approach to one's career is the experimental approach. Since business contexts will shift rapidly, as many professional functions may be irrelevant tomorrow, and since most companies will not reward loyalty, the approach is to get in, learn as much as one can, and move on. This is not only about self-protection and resilience. Gen Y is also teaching itself agility through constant personal experimentation—how not to be overly invested in any one choice, how not to get stuck professionally and emotionally. The twenty-first-century organization could certainly develop a lot more of this mind-set and be prepared to discard some of the incremental improvement mantras of the Industrial Revolution in favor of the exponential reinvention called for in the age of agility. But most organizations are plagued by an endemic fear of failure that paralyzes their ability even to trial experimentation.

I facilitated a webinar for about two hundred human resources directors, during which I issued a little poll asking, "What is your organization's attitude toward failure?" The results were as you might expect:

Anyone who fails is quickly fired.	**3 percent**
We never speak of failure—it's shameful.	**19 percent**
"Good" failure is tolerated but not shared.	**32 percent**
Failure is shared to a point, but there's still a stigma.	**43 percent**
Failure is shared and celebrated as important learning.	**3 percent**

The results demonstrate that businesses are in conflict with themselves. On one hand, the poll above reveals that 97 percent reported a range of mixed to negative organizational attitudes toward failure. On the other hand, 64 percent of the participants in this webinar told me that they absolutely must promote agility. Apparently, many leaders are not teaching by word or deed that an agile organization must also be a learning organization—one that embraces the insight from every opportunity tested, experiment run, win achieved, or customer lost. To do so, the company must always attempt new experiments, small changes, or game-changing ideas. In short, to win, you have to fail and not be afraid of failure.

If we look for them, the worlds of art and business are filled with stories of the virtue of overcoming the fear of failure and iterating one's way to success. Now, this is not to say that failure in and of itself is always a good thing. The point is that one must *control* the risk when experimenting to allow for as many prototypes and experiments as possible and in a manner that is economical based on whatever resources are most precious in one's context (money, time, people, etc.). The book *Art and Fear* tells of a ceramics teacher in the United States who split his students into two groups. One half would be graded on quantity—the number of pounds of ceramics produced by the end of the semester. The other half would be graded on quality, even if the work to be assessed was a single piece.

Contrary to what one might expect, the works of highest quality and design were all produced by the half of the class that was assessed for quantity. As the book's authors concluded, "It seems that while the 'quantity' group was busily churning out piles of work and learning from their mistakes, the 'quality' group had sat theorizing about perfection, and in the end had little more to show for their efforts than grandiose theories and a pile of dead clay."[18]

This experiment reveals that iteration and adaptation, rather than a one-off flash of genius-like inspiration, might ultimately produce the highest quality work, the best solution, or the finest creative output. Thomas Edison famously developed more than ten thousand prototypes of the light bulb, making both tiny and dramatic adjustments to his design each time, before he had a product that was elegant, reliable, and durable. Edison declared: "I have not failed ten thousand times. I have not failed once. I have succeeded in proving that those ten thousand ways will not work. When I have eliminated the ways that will not work, I will find the way that will work."[19]

Pixar, the digital animation production company with blockbusters including *Toy Story, Finding Nemo, WALL-E,* and *Up,* has enjoyed an unprecedented synergy of sustained commercial *and* critical success over many years. One might assume that Pixar employs genius writers who sit at home producing inspiring, funny screenplays, which they pop into the mail to Pixar headquarters in Emeryville, California, where the animators simply convert the complete stories into digital art. But this couldn't be further from the truth. New story lines at Pixar are just the starting point. Each bit of the story runs a gauntlet of multiple variations and rigorous debate among colleagues both inside and outside a given production team.

One of Pixar's ever-present practices is "Display."[20] If you are walking through the studios, you can't help but encounter work-in-progress, whether it's an open screening of the dailies of a film, or a gallery of character studies and storyboard drawings. These displays serve as an instant visual representation of the state of play, inviting everyone, even those just walking by, to contribute. Thinking of work as a state of perpetual beta and inviting comments, questions, and improvements facilitate learning, widen ownership of the problem, and ultimately lead to better output. All told, Pixar will often produce twelve thousand storyboard drawings to make one ninety-minute feature film.[21]

Ed Catmull, the president of Pixar and Walt Disney Animation Studios, very honestly assesses that Pixar's success comes down to constant challenge and revision: "Early on, all of our movies suck. That's a blunt assessment, I know, but I . . . choose that phrasing because saying it in a softer way fails to convey how bad the first versions of our films really are. I'm not trying to be modest or self-effacing by saying this. Pixar films are not good at first, and our job is to make them go . . . from suck to non-suck. We are true believers in the iterative process—reworking and reworking again, until a flawed story finds its through-line or a hollow character finds its soul."[22]

Andrew Stanton, Pixar's director of *Finding Nemo* and *WALL-E*, explains the company's creative process in a similar manner: "My strategy has always been: Be wrong as fast as we can, . . . which basically means, we're going to screw up. Let's just admit that. Let's not be afraid of that. You can't get to adulthood before you go through puberty. I won't get it right the first time, but I will get it wrong really soon, really quickly."[23]

The problem in how we think about creativity is that we only see the ultimate output—the beautiful ceramic pot, the stirring movie, the reliable light bulb. We focus on what we see, which is just the endpoint of a long iterative process. We even mistake how we get a flash of inspiration in our brains as a sudden act of creation, but the neuroscientist David Eagleman describes this flash as not an act of spontaneous genesis at all: "When an idea is served up from behind the scenes, the neural circuitry has been working on the problem for hours or days or years, consolidating information and trying out new combinations. But you merely take credit without further wonderment at the vast, hidden . . . machinery behind the scenes."[24]

These examples are not meant to entreat us to fail *per se*. Rather, they suggest a paradox that the creative process almost always involves trial and error, experiment and see, and iterative improvement. Organizations like Edison's, which later became known as a little company called General Electric, and Pixar have developed different methods to empower a necessary acceptance of failure along the inventive journey.[25]

Read enough literature on innovation and you swiftly come to the conclusion that one is more likely to succeed by imitating an acorn tree rather than a panda when it comes to creation. An acorn tree does not know where the ideal plot of ground is, where sunlight or water is ample. Therefore, it drops hundreds of acorns in as broad an area as possible in its act of creation. Similarly, the organization that tries many experiments is more likely to find successful game-changing ideas than the one that puts all its energy and resources into just one idea and one version of that idea. Unfortunately, most of our organizations approach experimentation in the same manner that pandas approach procreation. They attempt it with as little frequency as they possibly can, hoping for 100 percent success on a single try.

In order to control a proliferation of ideas and experiments, the innovative organization defines the parameters of the resources one may commit to the experiment, idea, or activity. For example, Google famously had a policy that its engineers could devote 20 percent of their time to personal projects. This resulted in some of Google's most successful products, including Gmail, AdSense, and Google Talk.[26] The lesson from Google is that agility is about how we act as much as about how we think. Allowing experimentation is a fantastic way to embed a growing culture of agility and innovation within the organization. As more people experiment, the more the company's culture resembles what it wishes to be. But successful experimentation relies on leaders shifting their attitude toward fail, and fail fast—the *learning* is paramount.

Beyond adopting the experimental approach on a personal level, what does experimentation look like on a business level? Can the Gen Y spirit to "get stuck in, learn, capitalize, and move on" actually help our companies grow their agility competence? I believe that it can, and there are some wonderful examples of organizations in the vanguard doing just that. Before we delve into those examples, let's define what a business experiment actually is: *A low-resource trial that tests a hypothesis, the goal of which is to uncover and share learning.* This is almost exactly how you would set up an experiment in a lab. You isolate one variable. You typically have a control sample and an experiment sample. You introduce one change, stimulus, or catalyst to the experiment sample and compare the results with those of the control sample.

Here are some examples to illustrate good hypotheses and how to test them. You'll notice that the hypotheses typically resemble if-then statements. The author of the hypothesis predicts an outcome and tests it by changing a single variable:

Everyday Experiments

Hypothesis	Control Group	Experiment Group	Controlling for the Variable
If I store my bananas in the refrigerator instead of on the kitchen counter, then they will last twice as long.	A bunch of bananas kept on the kitchen counter.	A bunch of bananas kept in the refrigerator.	Buy both bunches of bananas of equal quantity from the same store at the same time. Both bunches at the time of purchase should be at the same level of ripeness. Check each bunch daily and note if one bunch ripens earlier than the other. Does that trend continue with successive days?

(continues)

Hypothesis	Control Group	Experiment Group	Controlling for the Variable
If I give my houseplant more sunlight, then it will live longer.	Houseplant placed in a shady corner of the house.	Houseplant placed on a windowsill that receives a lot of sunlight.	Buy two of the same species of plants, of the same size and age, from the same store at the same time. Do not move the plants once you place them in the house. Give them the same amounts of water at the same times. Observe the health of the two plants over time. If one plant dies, note the date. When the other plant dies, note the date. As the only difference between the two plants was the amount of sunlight they received, then you can measure how many more days of life the sunlight provided.

Business Experiments

Hypothesis	Control Group	Experiment Group	Controlling for the Variable
If I automate the processing of orders, the cost of goods sold per order will decrease.	Note the call center average cost per order (status quo) for one product for one month.	Offer the same product to be purchased online for one month. Note the cost of building the online purchase form (and any variable costs).	Offer the same product, offered over the same month, sold via call center and online. Compare the two costs of goods sold at the end of the month.

Hypothesis	Control Group	Experiment Group	Controlling for the Variable
If I conduct a fun, team-building activity as part of our graduate intake induction, those new employees will be more engaged in their roles.	Issue an engagement survey to current graduate employees six months after their induction (status quo).	Run the team-building activity for the next intake's induction, and issue an engagement survey six months afterward.	Survey should be the same questions, issued in the same manner, after the same period of time after induction. Compare engagement scores.

Regardless of whether your hypothesis is proven or not, the point is that you now have more understanding of the opportunity or challenge that you are trying to crack. If your hypothesis is disproven, you try another variable with a new experiment, or simply move on. If, on the other hand, you prove your hypothesis, you may want to propose a business initiative, project, or change of course as a result of this newfound wisdom.

ROCHE'S GENIUS GEN Y EXPERIMENT

The Swiss pharmaceutical company Roche, the world's second largest biotech firm, at first glance would not be a candidate for agile experimentation. One would initially assume that Roche's competitive advantage is in its ability to scale innovation rather than to probe the boundaries of medicine's horizons. But Roche recognized that a "big corporate mind-set" would hinder its ability to innovate in the long term. This conclusion led to an intriguing question: Can the big corporate mind-set be disrupted by looking for game-changing ideas outside the company?

Through mastering experimentation as an everyday habit through an executive education program, a trio of Roche executives created a hypothesis to test this question: "By sourcing ideas from emerging scientists (students), the team would identify more promising opportunities." The concept embraced the innovation principle of crowdsourcing and the idea that great ideas don't always come from the longest-tenured stakeholders. Perhaps Gen Y researchers, accustomed to crowdsourced wisdom, would even enthusiastically participate?[27]

The Roche experiment team partnered with a corporate-university networking organization within their industry, the Oxbridge Biotech Roundtable. Students were encouraged to submit groundbreaking ideas that would tackle the most ambitious challenges or opportunities facing health care today. A handful of people with the best ideas would be invited to Basel, the company's headquarters, to present their concepts in greater detail, and the best idea would win a £5,000 (GBP) "Game Changing Innovation Prize." Note that the experiment was very low cost and would be completed in just a few months. Even if Roche did not acquire a brilliant new idea, it would learn one way or the other if crowdsourcing should be a usual approach to generating innovations.

In all, the team received 138 responses from students from 93 universities in 28 countries. Almost half of the ideas came from outside Roche's areas of core focus. The winner, from California, proposed a new product—3D bio-printed smart red blood cells—that was nowhere to be found in Roche's current research and development pipeline.

Regardless of whether this idea earns Roche even a single penny, the experiment team was 100 percent confident that their hypothesis was proven on the basis of the quality of several ideas they received. The experiment led to new business activity that was no longer in the category of "experimentation" but of "business as usual." The company decided it did need to operationalize and normalize engagement with the external university research world in order to mitigate an overly internal focus. According to Roche executive Sven Ebert, "What happens if the rules really change fundamentally somehow? We need to make sure our early-warning system is working well to make sure we stay relevant."[28]

A major conclusion that I have taken from facilitating business experiments with many clients is that it is vital the experiment is small, controlled, relatively quick to run, easy to conduct, and within the power of the person or group conducting the experiment to complete. *If managers perceive experiments as vast business projects that they will have to lead on top of their day jobs, and will require permission from others, the experiments will never see the light of day. An experiment is not a project. Its purpose is to produce a learning outcome.* If an experiment yields sufficient knowledge that leads to a project, then the company can more confidently allocate resources to that project since the outcome is more predictable. The organization thereby readily embraces agility because its experimentation activity de-risks innovation.

Just like conducting experiments in a lab, we can only guess what variable is the critical one, what stimulus will produce a desired result. Therefore, we need to discard the notion that, as managers, we are all-wise and our first, best guess is necessarily the correct one. We need to conduct dozens or even hundreds of experiments throughout the organization all the time. We want to learn as quickly and as constantly as we can. That's only possible through leveraging the power of volume. By testing many hypotheses and many variables within each hypothesis, organizations by priority and habit embrace learning and therefore foster and nurture inspiration, and finally evolve into the agile first-movers that are the terror and pride of their industries. In making experimentation an organizational habit, the companies at the vanguard of embracing the habits of agility are more likely to invent the future rather than to be victimized by it.

INSIGHTS TO ACTIONS
One Thing You Can Do Monday Morning

Run an experiment to start exercising your own agility muscles. Create a hypothesis and test it. Remember that a hypothesis is a prediction of the outcome of a test. It forms the basis of designing an experiment. A good hypothesis must be provable, meaning it makes a prediction that you can test. Your experiment will then demonstrate if your prediction was accurate or not. As an aide-mémoire, here are a couple more good, testable hypotheses:

- ► Employees who sleep at least seven hours a night are more productive than those who do not.
- ► Sales staff who have at least one face-to-face customer meeting per day have a higher conversion rate than those who do not.

In creating your own hypothesis, ask yourself: What do you wonder about that, if true, would have a business benefit to you, your team, or your organization? Then ask yourself: What assumptions might you be making that, if proven or disproven, would have a business benefit?

Once you have a hypothesis, create a short, easy, time-bound experiment to assess its validity. How would you test it? What's the comparator or control? Would you need anyone else to help you conduct the experiment? Who? For how long?

Remember that whether your hypothesis is disproven or not, the key output of the experiment is to gain insight from which you can then act with confidence to enhance your or your team's effectiveness. Once you're comfortable practicing the experimental method, teach your colleagues and make experimentation a way of life in your company.

10

PURPOSE—THE POWER OF A STRONG, SHARED "WHY"

Got to find out
Don't want to wait
Got to make sure that my life will be great
Got to find my purpose before it's too late
—PRINCETON, *Avenue Q*[1]

Psychologist Abraham Maslow, the creator of the well-known Maslow's hierarchy of needs,[2] wrote, "To know what one really wants is a considerable psychological achievement."[3] Just as this argument is true for individuals, it can only be healthy for companies occasionally to review if they are still relevant, fit for purpose, and if their purpose itself should be confronted and reenergized. When organizations do this well, there is an injection of energy and focus in its employees that is also infectious in customers and investors. Purpose-driven leadership is critical to most Gen Ys, and is also the quality they would most wish to emulate as they assume leadership positions in their own right.

Facebook's human resources team investigated what their Gen Y population sought from their employer and confirmed that purpose matters enormously. After surveying their workforce twice a year and seeking the major themes from hundreds of thousands of responses, Facebook identified three categories that contribute most to their people's motivation. These groupings are similar but not identical to Maslow's hierarchy. They call these three buckets "career, community and cause." Career is about enjoying a healthy degree of autonomy, the ability to apply one's strengths, and the opportunity to grow; this is about intrinsic motivation. Community is about experiencing respect, care, and recognition from one's colleagues; this is about connection and belonging. Cause is about purpose, making an impact and believing in the organization's mission; this is about pride in what you do.[4] We might ask ourselves at this point, "What is the most important area?" And if we don our futurist hat, "What matters most to the Gen Y leader for his or her own people?"

To look deeper into that future and explore how our companies may change as Gen Ys enter the executive suite, I asked a final question in my survey of Gen Y high potentials introduced in chapter 1: "What would be your focus if you were the leader of your organization?" In other words, what would be your mantra, your daily guiding light, if you were the CEO? They had five general options, and I asked participants to select only their most preferred answer. The options speak to five themes: minding one's core business KPIs (Key Performance Indicators, such as same-store sales), going global, thinking entrepreneurially, aligning with purpose, and maximizing financial return.[5] I anticipated a spread of choices across these options and wondered if a favorite would emerge. The results were most startling and demonstrate a clear shift to new paradigms over the theory and practice of leadership in the twentieth century.

**What would be your
focus if you were the leader of your organization?**

Focus on how business is trading   **11.5 percent**

Focus on the global growth of the business	**11.5 percent**
Focus on an entrepreneurial perspective	**33 percent**
Focus on renewing personal and organizational mission	**43 percent**

If you were doing your own sums of these percents, you noticed that there's still a miniscule fraction of the survey-takers remaining. The tiny response to this final option is deafeningly profound in its departure from traditional wisdom:

Focus on the financial worth of the business	**1 percent**

This result demonstrates a seismic shift away from the twentieth century paradigm that the only purpose of a company, and by extension its leader, is to maximize profit and return to shareholders. Only two decades ago, this idea would have been considered commonsensical, reinforced by every CEO and finance professor. Now don't get me wrong—of course companies should keep their shareholders' interests in mind. But much of the corporate malfeasance of the past thirty-odd years, at its core, was rooted in executives' ignoring the needs of their stakeholders—those responsible for creating and purchasing the value that the company produces from its products and services. I will explore this theme in more detail in the next chapter.

Spending time on embedding purpose in an organization is not only about focusing on the value the organization contributes to customers, how it serves unmet or poorly met needs, but also empowers employees to own the brand in their daily activity, to be more conscious and proactive in being stewards of value, and to connect what they do to why they do it. "The contract between the organization and the individual is beginning to change," says Professor Lynda Gratton of London Business School. "The old contract looked like this: 'I work to buy stuff that makes me happy.' The contract is negotiated by tangible assets. The new contract will be, 'I work to make me happy.' We have to think about work as being the thing, not the money you get from it. I don't see many companies realizing how profound that change will be."[6]

The company that has a strongly articulated, values-driven purpose, which is seen to deliver on a daily basis, will win the talent war, recruiting its first-choice candidates and retaining them longer than their competitors. It is not only my own survey that demonstrates the import of purpose in Gen Y's selection of employers. According to research at Princeton University, more than 85 percent of young people claim that their number one criterion in seeking an employer is meaning and a strong sense of purpose.[7] As important, research by Bain & Company discovered that those employees working for purpose-driven companies are more than three times more productive than their dissatisfied counterparts.[8] Different sources are converging on the conclusion that purpose delivers manifold benefits, among them attraction, engagement, and effectiveness.

After all, is it reasonable to expect that customers will be well served if one's employees are not? Based on this correlation, Vineet Nayar, the former CEO of Indian IT services company HCL Technologies, declared to his people, "Employees first, customers second!" This clarion call also became the title of Nayar's book.[9] Colleagues must serve one another with the same focus as if they were customers themselves, and in developing good habits, such as creating and fulfilling service tickets even for internal questions or requests, the organization builds an ethos that translates into world-class products and services for its customers.

HARVESTING PURPOSE AT FRUCOR SUNTORY

Sarah Langley, Suntory's deputy COO for global human resources, identified that a powerful retention tool for young employees is how the organization fulfils its mission: "To create harmony with people and nature," and its vision, "Growing for good." She explains: "We have to be more lined up around doing good for society versus getting drinks in the hands of consumers. So, we have to be more overt about community, sugar, water use and landfill, for example." Salary, on the other hand, is usually not as strong a tool: "It's only a hygiene factor. Salary is less relevant than it used to be."[10]

Sarah is quick to point out that human resources does not have to manage all the company's corporate social responsibility (CSR) initiatives. Rather, she gives that privilege to those who are most passionate to drive these activities. Suntory aims to nurture the whole person, and a degree of autonomy toward how its employees grow and develop is a simple but effective step in that direction. Sarah summarizes, "Our most effective managers . . . look for opportunities and challenges to grow back their people." This is the first time I've heard the phrase "grow back." It is a twist on "give back" and implies a social contract whereby managers are obliged to grow their people, but also that those direct reports have a responsibility to create their own opportunities as well. The organization is enriched when those opportunities are derived from individuals' personal and professional purpose.

Those who initiate CSR projects must set tangible goals and be sure to share what they're doing internally and externally. Not only are these projects good for enhancing employees' and customers' goodwill, but the company benefits in that leading the projects enhances relevant skills among their people, such as project management, interpersonal capability, cross-functional collaboration, adaptability, and resilience. Given the rise of funding in the not-for-profit sector, salaries for managers of charities are becoming competitive with those in the commercial sector. Suntory recognizes, therefore, that doing good for their communities is ever more critical in order to retain their own people.

Langley mentions Frucor Suntory as a good example of this self-starting CSR activity. She was previously the chief people officer of Frucor, the Australasian nonalcoholic drinks company and market leader for energy drinks that was acquired by Suntory in 2009. One of the community initiatives that just a few colleagues started at the renamed Frucor Suntory is "Kiwi Harvest," which rescues foodstuffs that would have gone to waste and distributes them to those in need throughout New Zealand. Communicating Kiwi Harvest to the wider organization was important because, first, even those not involved felt more engaged with their company, knowing the organization is motivated to be a force for good. Talking about the project with customers also became a strong relationship builder, and many of these retailers have donated food and drink to Kiwi Harvest.

Second, more people ultimately got involved, even if they were not initially part of the project team. Kiwi Harvest depends on the company's delivery drivers believing in this project. After all, without a distribution mechanism, the initiative would fail quickly. Drivers became involved beyond transporting the foods and have also been involved in fundraising and food drives to enhance the scale of the program. Today, every employee can volunteer, which may include helping a driver on the road or packing food at the warehouse. Frucor Suntory's progressive people agenda is putting the lie to the stereotype of the salaryman with no time for community or family. It turns out that nurturing the whole person is not only good for employees but for all those in their orbits.

If it is a reasonable expectation today that a company considers how to live its purpose, the preceding step would be that it articulates a clear, actionable, shared, and agreed purpose in the first place. How does one go about this? I will share my own approach, refined through years of iteration with my own corporate clients.

CREATING AND ALIGNING PURPOSE

In addition to adding value to employees in everyday life, creating and articulating purpose is a conscious act, one best approached with dedicated time and thoughtfulness. What constitutes performing this exercise well is keeping it authentic: lots of discussions, focus groups, asking hard questions, resolving contradictions, integrating the hopes and aspirations at all levels of the company and among all critical stakeholders, be they internal or external. At its worst, this is merely a public relations exercise delivered by high-priced communications consultants and/or the shareholder relations department, and is articulated only through the lens of "what sounds good" instead of "How will this guide behavior?"

It is always a good idea to revisit one's corporate purpose every now and then. I have worked with companies who have not reflected on their guiding principles since their founding . . . some hundred-plus years ago! With constant industry disruption becoming the norm, it is ever more crucial to keep returning to the question, "Are we as relevant as we can possibly be today?" One of the reasons that start-ups seem to have the disruption advantage over their incumbent competitors is that the entrepreneurs have freshly explored the question of their own relevance. A start-up begins and ends every day asking itself if it has progressed in finding its place in the world. The incumbent has the scale advantage but frequently cedes the relevance space to its nimbler opponents.

The approach I will outline can be facilitated with groups as small as four and as large as one hundred. I cannot stress enough that, regardless of the size of the group, you must devote adequate time to the exercise—at least a full day. The temptation may be to try to accelerate the process: "Why not just be super-efficient and do it in half a day?" I've found that to do so is counterproductive for several reasons.

First, while you may reach the point where all ideas in the room are captured, the rushed nature of the exercises will mean that you will not have true buy-in from the group; everyone will have dutifully completed the exercises in the time allotted, but it will become about task completion rather than shared agreement that everyone can get behind these answers.

Second and related point, the day is not only about capturing ideas. You will require at least as much time to discuss which ideas the group will willingly advocate as you spent generating those ideas in the first place.

Third, you need the time to draw out multiple views. If you rush, the extroverted personalities and/or the most senior people in the room will jump in with their ideas, and the introverts and their junior colleagues will defer. But silence does not imply assent; it might simply mean that some people were not given adequate time or space to share their opinions.

Finally, and perhaps it goes without saying, the participants in this exercise must include those with the authority and influence to align the company around the decisions made during the day but should not solely involve these people.

Now that we've sorted some of the principles of success for this day, here is one suggestion, a facilitator's guide if you will, for how to bring your people together around a strong, clear, shared understanding of "why we do what we do," and, more important, how that understanding informs behaviors, decisions, strategy, priorities, and culture.

A DAY OF PURPOSE

Take some time to allow people to get to know one another outside of work. A little bit of investment in this exercise up front will pay dividends later, as colleagues will relate to one another just as human beings, sharing what they really think rather than "what they're supposed to say." One simple exercise that I have always found effective and fun, regardless of the seniority and seriousness of the groups, is to ask everyone to find the person in the room that he or she knows least well. In pairs, each person spends a minute telling the other a story about him or herself that will impress, surprise, shock, or disgust(!), but the story cannot be from or about work. If time allows, I usually then ask everyone to pair up with another partner—again, someone they don't know well. This time, each person tells the other what they are proudest of (OTHER than their children, which is too easy), or maybe their best or most memorable moment from the past year. I'm attempting to humanize the group very quickly with these exercises, sharing stories from our lives outside of our careers, so that everyone sees the other beyond title or track record in the company. I often then ask a couple of people to share a story they heard from their partners, which usually solicits a lot of heartfelt laughs and surprises.

Now that the group is warmed up, and warmed to one another, explain that purpose operates on a number of levels, that an organization at any point in its evolution and based on its context today may require a purpose that expands its ambition or constrains its focus.[11] If the former, ambition may be required, because the organization has undersold the impact it can make, that its capability or know-how is widely relevant to other customers, geographies, applications, or partners. If the latter, the company may have overly diluted its resources, trying to do too much or cover too much ground, where more value or better service could be offered with a little more restraint on the organization's frenzy of activity. At this point, it's worth a discussion as to whether the group thinks its company's purpose needs to be more expansive or more focused.

Two other levels on which you may discuss purpose are "who we are" and "where we are going." I've seen too many conversations run off the rails because the participants were simultaneously discussing purpose on both of these levels, but not distinguishing when they were talking about one or the other, leading to confusion and frustration on all sides. It really needs to be two separate though equally useful explorations. Therefore, I've separated these exercises for this day.

Who We Are

A smooth channel into organizational identity is to start with values. If your company has never articulated its values, you have a greenfield opportunity here. If your company has declared values, particularly long-held, venerated ones, this exercise may actually be tougher because you may be probing and perhaps challenging sacred cows. Either way, don't avoid this exercise. Even if your company has its values chiseled into the lobby walls, how were these values decided? Who codified them and when? Too often, values were not an exercise of the community, but a project completed by a communications or marketing agency for investors and analysts—just a piece of honeyed word-smithery.

If your organization has not defined its values, begin by asking everyone to write down every word they can think of that can be used to describe the company—only one word for each entry, though they can be nouns or adjectives. Request that each word is written on a separate sticky note. Give them at least ten minutes to do this piece, because once everyone has written the obvious words, they often surface descriptors that may have only been subconscious before this day.

Stick a very large and wide piece of blank paper (I often use butcher paper) on the wall. Draw a line horizontally across the entire page about one-third from the bottom of the paper. On the far left, draw a "+" and "-" symbol, indicating positive and negative. Draw three vertical lines, dividing the paper into three equal areas. Across the top of each of these areas, write the following labels: EMPLOYEES, CUSTOMERS, PUBLIC. When you are finished, your paper should look like this:

	EMPLOYEES	CUSTOMERS	PUBLIC
+			
-			

If you have more than fifty participants, you may want to have two posters in the room. Now ask everyone to come up to the poster and place their sticky notes in the relevant area: negative words in the bottom row, positive words in the larger area above. Participants should also consider which stakeholder group (employees, customers, public[12]) would be most likely to use each of their words and place their sticky note under that label. All the same words should be clustered together. If identical words appear in different boxes, move all of those words to the most popular box, as this would be the consensus view. As people are putting up their sticky notes, encourage them to speak to one another about why they chose these words and placed them in these categories. These informal conversations are often more honest and unguarded, as no one is on the spot speaking to the entire room.

As the facilitator, you may want to call a break here to clean up the posters, making sure that the same or very similar words are clustered together and that words are appropriately identified as positive or negative descriptors. Put decidedly neutral words on the line between "+" and "-". The room has now effectively created a heat map, where the largest clusters represent the most widely held opinions.

When you reconvene after the exercise, have a conversation about the story the poster is telling. What is our collective voice saying about this organization? What are our strengths and weaknesses? Remove those sticky notes that radically differ from the consensus in the room. Remove all the negative words in the bottom row. This row was useful in allowing everyone to contribute every descriptor they could conceive without editing themselves. Quantity yields better quality, as we have already discovered! Once you're through the obvious deletions, you can then start to make harder decisions and eliminate more words that feel true for some but not for most. If you have synonyms, as a room decide which word feels truest and remove the others. Ultimately, you want no more than six to eight words remaining, with at least one or two under the stakeholder columns of "Public" and "Customers."

Now discuss which words are completely accurate in terms of how we would describe ourselves today and which ones are more aspirational. You may want to discuss "aspirational" in two manners: First, who are we at our best? How do we hope to talk about ourselves if we grow in our success and esteem? Second, which aspirational words are compelling because they are the opposite of some of the consensus negative words we had on the poster? Over time, if these aspirational words grow in feeling authentic, it would mean we have worked on those parts of our character that bother us today. Finally, take your final six to eight words and write them as a large vertical list on the wall, with those words that are most true today at the bottom and most aspirational at the top.[13] Have one final conversation if any of these words feel a little off the mark, inauthentic, or uninspiring. Remove any that do not meet this test. What remains are your four to six values.

If your organization has defined its values already, it may be first worth asking the room if people know what they are (too frequently, no one has a clue!), and how and when they were created. If no one in the room can claim any responsibility for participating in the process, then I recommend starting again. Either way, complete the exercise we've just defined, but include the current values on the poster. When you begin the process of elimination and draw your ladder of aspiration, you will discover that some of the older values no longer resonate and have been replaced with more moving, true, or exciting values. It's perfectly valid to ask, "Is this value no longer as relevant?" No matter the answer, you would have already enhanced the engagement and affiliation of employees to their company because they have at last had the invaluable opportunity to participate in their professional community's identity.

At this point, your participants may be asking themselves, "OK, so what do we do now that we've identified our values going forward?" It's a good point; no one wants this exercise to be an academic one, which has no bearing on actual organizational life. If you believe the argument (and I hope you do) that values inform behaviors, behaviors define culture, and culture affects how colleagues interact with one another and with customers, then the next step is to help the group bridge the gap between values and behaviors. If a group of influential and/or senior colleagues has a shared understanding of what behaviors will help them to succeed and win in the marketplace, survive and get things done internally, and proactively practice those behaviors consistently, then others will emulate those behaviors, consciously or unconsciously. Most new or junior employees enter a company and look around for those who are successful and imitate the behaviors they observe in those people. It's only natural, and we've been doing this since we were children. As we observed in chapter 4, culture is simply shared behaviors. It's not overly complicated.

To achieve this alignment, at this point in the workshop, encourage the room to break into small groups and list a couple of behaviors that would be consistent and observable for each value that made the final list. You could also assign one value to each group or table to do this exercise. Ask each group to share its brainstorm. Now discuss with the room which one behavior you heard that would most either reinforce or create that value. It's important to be quite disciplined in reducing the behaviors to one, maybe two, for each value, or no one will remember how they are actually supposed to practice those values.

To ensure that your people will actually practice the agreed behaviors, in order to embed the values in the days and months to come, I like to ask everyone at this point to pair with someone with whom they work, ideally colocated, on at least a fairly regular basis. They will act as a peer support pair, holding each other to account if they are not observing the agreed behaviors, or worse, doing the opposite of the desired behavior—acting counterculturally. I ask the pairs to agree on a regular rhythm to check in with each other, perhaps every other week, and share feedback. Of course, it's also an opportunity to ask one's peer for help if one is struggling. There's certainly no shame in this. In many cases, to request a different behavior of senior leaders is to ask them to change habits formed over many decades. It may not happen overnight, and it definitely requires regular, front-of-mind, attention.

It's vital to know who you are as a company, how you work together, and how you add value to customers. As Western economies transition more to creative and professional service industries, "how" a company delivers its services is fundamental. In many cases the "how" is the only meaningful differentiator among competitors. Consider, for example, two retail banks offering mortgages with identical terms and interest rates. A customer would most likely choose one mortgage provider over the other based on the service they receive, and, more accurately, what type of service matters most to that customer. This service is distinguished by the character of those banks, informed by their values, and manifested in their employees' behaviors. In short, knowing who you are as a company matters.

You've now spent perhaps half a day agreeing on who you are: your values and what those values look like in practice (behaviors). You have invited your colleagues to support one another in their commitment to role model the behaviors that manifest the values. It's time to turn your attention to the other lens of organizational purpose—where you are going.

Where We Are Going

After lunch, your group is hopefully raring for more Purpose. The focus for the afternoon is on our journey, gaining clarity on the path, commitment to take that path, and a consistent story to tell others about why we're taking this journey.

I prefer to start this exploration with the long-term view. What is our destination ten or even twenty years from now? You could call this your "vision," if you prefer. One exercise I love to facilitate here is first to break the room into groups of about four or five people, then to ask each group to pretend that we have time-traveled twenty years into the future and to compose a simple two- to three-minute presentation for shareholders or for the company internally on what we have achieved and how we reached the pinnacle of success that we now enjoy. I leave it to the groups if they want to create any visual aids, slides, and so on.

As the groups present, ask everyone else to note down anything they hear that is powerfully compelling, that is worthy of the company's time, and that would sustain employees' engagement and focus long term. As the facilitator, note on a poster any common themes you hear. After the final presentation, lead a conversation about: Where is the shared vision? Is it compelling? Can we all agree to this?

There is a fine line here between ambitious and realistic. I would err on the side of ambitious. As the destination is very long term, it should be a substantial, toothsome vision, perhaps even one that may not ever be 100 percent achieved but is nevertheless worthy of pursuit. The impact of the vision should generate tremendous excitement, even if it were mostly but not fully realized. This long term vision is ideally no more than one sentence. It must be pithy enough to inspire instant recall. Here are a few examples of visions that I particularly like:

NIKE: To bring innovation and inspiration to every athlete in the world[14];

GOOGLE/ALPHABET: To organize the world's information and make it universally accessible and useful[15];

AMAZON: To be Earth's most customer-centric company, where customers can come to find and discover anything they might want to buy online.[16]

This can be quite a tough, perhaps emotional, conversation, particularly if there's disagreement about where people want to take the organization. At the same time, take solace that, if this is the case, this conversation had to happen, and sooner rather than later. Corporate strategy relies on a common understanding of the destination, as the vision informs decisions, priorities, and how resources are allocated. Just as we translated values into behaviors, we follow the same approach converting the destination into medium- and short-term choices.

You may have depleted both the time allocated for the day and the energy of the group. If so, then proceed to the next exercise the following day. If not, then this final exercise should take up the remaining two hours or so of your day's agenda. Write the vision that you have just agreed on in large print on the wall. Divide the room into groups of four to five people. Ask each group to discuss, debate, and agree on one strategic action with a three- to five-year time frame, which, if achieved, would give everyone confidence that the company is on the right track to achieve its long-term vision. Unlike the vision (the destination), this strategic action is very specific: 1) There is a stated objective; 2) There is a plan to achieve that objective; 3) You would know that the objective has been achieved (implying that the objective is measurable); and 4) You have a target time by when the objective should be achieved.

Here are some examples of such strategic actions. I have not included the plan to achieve the objectives due to confidentiality:

A business school: To be in the *Financial Times* top five combined rankings in three years;

An FMCG company: To deliver double-digit earnings growth and touch two hundred million new customers every year for the next five years;

A commercial real estate agency: To win the dominant share of top ten opportunities by 2017.

Ask each group to present their strategic action to the room and lead a discussion as to which one we can get behind. It's best to achieve focus and therefore to converge on just one, though this does not imply that the company would not pursue a number of activities in relation to its strategy. Consider the following criteria in deciding which strategic action to choose:

1. Is the objective achievable?
2. Is it achievable within three to five years?
3. Is the path to achieve the objective realistic and doable, i.e., there are no technological, structural, or regulatory reasons why we cannot embark on this activity immediately?
4. Do we agree that if we achieve this objective, then we are clearly and firmly on the right path to achieve the long-term vision to which we have just committed?
5. Do we all agree that this is a compelling, energizing strategic action?

There is one final exercise that I prefer to run on a Purpose day, particularly if the participants in the room are heads of function or have their own earnings responsibilities. Ask everyone to pair up and have a conversation about the following: How will you and your team contribute to achieving the strategic action that we have just agreed on? Be as specific as possible. What's the activity? Who is doing it? How are they doing it? When will it be done? It's crucial that the time frame to begin the team's contribution to the strategic action is quick, a couple of weeks at the most. Otherwise, it is far too easy for the entire collective commitment to wither on the vine from conditions like, "I'm too busy with the day job," or "I'll get started when I see others get started," or plain old ennui.

The final question for the listener in the peer pair is, "How can I support you?" I ask each pair to pull out their phones (the only time this is allowed) to find a time to catch up, in no more than a month, and share how they are progressing and if they could use further support, advice, or cover from their colleague.

If time allows, I ask each person even to rehearse with her peer how she will share the outputs of this Purpose day with her team when she returns to the office. How will she facilitate a discussion around the purpose and what the implications are for us as a team and as individuals? How will she share the strategic action, why is it important, how will she increase excitement for this commitment, how will she keep the conversation on track rather than tip into a

whining session about how this is just more work? The listener can
assist her partner by role playing a team member and asking questions that she anticipates receiving.

Certainly, the company will have to flesh out the tactics, timeline,
and resources to commit to the strategic action in the days to
come after this workshop. The important objective is that everyone
knows and agrees the strategic action. In doing so, the entire organization can comprehend not only the refreshed vision but is confident
that there is a plan to achieve it and that there are clear milestones.
Embedding those markers into everyone's professional objectives, at
every level, and celebrating when we reach those markers, keeps the
organization focused on its higher-level purpose.

Usually when it comes to purpose, there are two camps. I'll just
call them "old schoolers" and "progressives." The former group
believes that business is solely about making money, and the
whole "purpose" malarkey is a distraction, composed by a cottage
industry of consultants and former summer camp counselors
with guitars at the ready under their desks. The latter group considers not only the benefit of a strong, shared purpose, but recognizes that there are compelling reasons why a CEO would want
his or her people excited enough about their mission that they
consistently contribute exceptional discretionary effort, demonstrate that they prioritize correctly in service of the company's
highest-level goals, and know how and why they personally create
value for their customers and stakeholders, regardless of their
functions. Because of this focus, those organizations who embrace the latter camp tend dramatically to outperform the former, despite their so-called hard-nosed focus on the bottom line,
when it comes to earnings or share price. In the next chapter,
we'll explore the evidence for this state of affairs.

●　　●　　●

INSIGHTS TO ACTIONS
One Thing You Can Do Monday Morning

This would be more ambitious than one Monday morning activity, but I hope you would consider facilitating a workshop with your team along the lines of that outlined in this chapter. Far too many employees cannot say either what their organization's purpose is or that they can see that purpose realized in their day-to-day efforts. I personally believe it is the employer's and the manager's responsibility to ensure that they can help their people draw a line explicitly between their personal purpose and that of their company.

One-to-ones between line managers and direct reports are usually about reviewing performance against objectives and key performance indicators, and/or maybe a bit of "How's it going?" As an alternative, consider meeting with your reports and asking questions such as: "What is it about work that makes you happiest?" "Tell me why you chose to work here instead of anywhere else?" "Why did you choose this profession?" "What is the greatest imaginable impact you would wish to have through your work?" In asking your people to talk more about why they do this job *and* identify what the company does which is of value to them, they begin to make a connection between the personal and collective missions. It then becomes easier over time to discuss wide themes such as mission, purpose, vision and for teams to discuss more openly and vulnerably what they hope for in return for their labor beyond their daily bread. All research indicates that such dialogue contributes strongly to recruitment, culture, loyalty, and engagement.

11

FINANCIAL IMPLICATIONS OF NEXT GENERATION LEADERSHIP

With great power comes great responsibility.
—VOLTAIRE (and Spider-Man's Uncle Ben)[1]

Gen Y comprises fully half of the American workforce today and by 2025 will be 75 percent of the global workforce.[2] This is a critical mass who demands a shift that we are just starting to observe from shareholder to stakeholder capitalism. It is essentially a rebalance in corporate focus from outcomes to outputs. If we think of outcomes as share price and profit, we cannot deny that these are good things to have. But I can't storm into the office and say that my focus today will be to maximize my share price. What am I supposed to do? A blinkered focus on share price creates drift away from the reasons a company was founded in the first place: to identify a market need and to serve customers brilliantly. Creating value for customers and serving them better are outputs that companies can rally behind and can guide whether to spend more time on activity A or activity B. My outputs will lead to the outcome of enhancing my bottom line. But the outcome is not my daily focus—this is a subtle but hugely important point.

Returning to my original Gen Y survey, where I asked what Yers would focus on if they were the CEOs of their organizations, here are their answers again[3]:

What would be your focus if you were the leader of your organization?

Focus on how business is trading	**11.5 percent**
Focus on the global growth of the business	**11.5 percent**
Focus on an entrepreneurial perspective	**33 percent**
Focus on renewing personal and organizational mission	**43 percent**
Focus on the financial worth of the business	**1 percent**

On the occasions when I have shared these responses with audiences, I always follow up by asking if the last response, the 1 percent, scares them. Usually the audience is about fifty-fifty "scared, not scared." I would posit that if 50 percent of a population is scared about a topic, then it's worthy of attention. Either way, that 1 percent is significant in its insignificance—that "financial worth" bears so little import to this Gen Y population. This answer flies in the face of conventional wisdom that the purpose of business is to maximize profit and shareholder return.

Does this mean that the Gen Y CEO would not want to earn a profit? Absolutely not. Business has to survive and thrive. Here's the rub. Most businesses (yes, even banking) started because of a strong sense of purpose: introducing an exciting product to the world, serving a previously undiscovered market need, bettering a community, creating employment opportunities. But then financial analysts' opinions grew in importance to investors, with their use of various ratios that are useful shortcuts in assessing company health. However, we must remember that these shortcuts are only performance indicators for today; they do not assess if the business is closer to or further from achieving its purpose, closer to or further from achieving long-term and "moon shot" objectives.

Chasing ratio optimization is a short-term game. Before one knows it, the purpose of the business is about tacitly, implicitly pleasing analysts. Making decisions toward long-term objectives takes a back seat. If the CEO or CFO starts adopting someone else's KPIs, using these analyst ratios as their primary KPIs, they risk creating drift from the mission of the organization. Over time, this can make sustained success much harder. Unfortunately, that's exactly what happened on a massive scale.

At an inflection point in the second half of the twentieth century, as analysts' and shareholders' voices became louder, the CFOs and investor relations' departments began to dominate the C-suite conversations. CEOs' compensations grew increasingly related to share price and less on customer value indicators. The focus on outputs dropped down the totem pole in terms of time and attention in favor of outcomes. One could argue that the Great Recession of 2007–09 was caused, or at least made much worse, by this shift in focus by too many corporations.

Enron's demise is a story that brings into sharp focus why it is necessary to prevent the egregiously irresponsible activities that emerge when executives spend all day, every day, vainly trying to manipulate outcomes. Enron was a company as traditional as it comes—an electricity and gas supplier. Sixty years after its founding, though, its focus looked more like that of a hedge fund than of a commodity supplier, reinvesting its profits in other investment products, hedge and arbitrage activities, and (most notably) squirreling away losses in offshore accounts. *Fortune* magazine awarded Enron the title of "America's Most Innovative Company" for six years in a row, from 1996 to 2001. Ironically, in hindsight, Enron's creativity reached its apex in its accounting practices. As the obsession to maximize the outcome, the share price, reached maniacal heights, its attention to its core outputs—its products, services, and customers—plummeted in equal measure.[4] While Chairman Kenneth Lay and CEO Jeff Skilling were both convicted of conspiracy, fraud, and insider trading, the real losers were Enron's customers, partners, and suppliers, many of whom trusted the company almost to the bitter end. Enron's story in a wider perspective is the tale of how the practice of shareholder capitalism, stretched to its endgame, lost its relevance as a force for good.

We're now on the threshold of stakeholder capitalism—a vigorous focus on customers and employees first. And thank goodness that Gen Ys have their priorities right, placing outputs over outcomes, focusing on renewing and strengthening their purpose in everyday activities. Gen Ys are leading the way in reinventing capitalism that serves society better and more widely.

As one example, take a look at Facebook, founded and led by one of the first Gen Y Fortune 500 CEOs, Mark Zuckerberg. Now, I would be the first to admit that Facebook is far from perfect, but its early history as a publicly traded company and how it catalyzed investor confidence is a thought-provoking case study. In his letter to prospective shareholders as part of the company's initial public offer in 2012, Zuckerberg did not emphasize revenue and profit forecasts. Instead, he explained Facebook's purpose and simply stated that if you believed in that goal then you might consider investing. Zuckerberg wrote: "Facebook was not originally created to be a company. It was built to accomplish a social mission—to make the world more open and connected. We think it's important that everyone who invests in Facebook understands what this means to us, how we make decisions and why we do the things we do. I will try to outline our approach in this letter."[5]

This simple little note sent shock waves through the analyst community. Such a pitch was almost unheard of. What is the poor investment researcher to do with this information? Consider that the best-practice standard for a letter to shareholders had to this point resembled something much more like the typical opening paragraph from a guru such as the "Oracle of Omaha," CEO and chairman of conglomerate Berkshire Hathaway, Warren Buffett. Look at how Buffett began a shareholder note at about the same time that Zuckerberg composed his own: "Berkshire's gain in net worth during 2013 was $34.2 billion. That gain was after deducting $1.8 billion of charges. . . . The per-share book value of both our Class A and Class B stock increased by 18.2 percent. Over the last forty-nine years (that is, since present management took over), book value has grown from $19 to $134,973, a rate of 19.7 percent compounded annually."[6] The analyst practically shivers with delight when handed all the figures and forecasts that one could need to produce lovely and colorful graphs for asset managers and individual investors alike.

We might think that Zuckerberg's approach was naïve, and that shareholder capital would not congregate in Facebook's coffers, that it flocks only to those companies selling the classic "hockey stick" income graph. But we would be wrong. Facebook shareholders earned 100 percent return on investment year-on-year in the company's first three years of being publicly traded, essentially doubling one's investment every year.

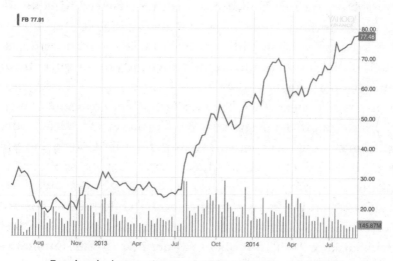

Facebook share price, June 2012 to September 2014[7]

In comparison, consider that the ten-year average return for the S&P 500 index over the past ninety years is but 9.8 percent.[8] Any investor would have killed for such an asset as Facebook in its first three years of going public. Even later, and despite negative publicity in 2017, Facebook still outperformed most Fortune 500 companies, delivering a rocking 53.4 percent return in that single year.[9]

Don't get me wrong: I have no problem with Berkshire Hathaway as an investment. In fact, in full disclosure, I'm a shareholder myself. The point is that comparing the approach of Buffett to Zuckerberg demonstrates that the Gen Y purpose-driven focus does not necessarily produce a trade-off with financial results. In fact, such focus sometimes produces superior results!

We cannot conclude that Facebook's return on investment during this period was only possible because the organization was young and scrappy. Whether we are comparing start-ups, unicorns, or stalwarts, we find that companies who make the conscious evolution toward a purpose-driven ethos are also typically rewarded for it by their employees, customers, and investors. For the past nine years, global consumer goods giant Unilever has shifted its attention toward social and environmental goals: Do good for your community and planet and good things will happen. More precisely, Unilever's executives are incentivized to advance its social responsibility agenda,[10] a simple step that is nevertheless radically different from most companies who include social responsibility in their rhetoric yet only incentivize financial performance.

In a span of nine years, Unilever's employee engagement metrics have improved 60 percent, and Unilever has become the third most desirable company to work for after Google and Apple.[11] If HCL Technologies' Vineet Nayar's hypothesis is correct that to focus on employees also benefits customers and shareholders, then Unilever is another poster child for this positive correlation. As of this writing, Unilever's share price has almost doubled since 2010, from about $27 per share to $52. Employees and shareholders are delighted in equal measure.

Unilever has also famously tried to break this analyst-driven, short-term dynamic by informing the investor community that it will no longer publish quarterly forecasts. The intention was entirely to allow former CEO Paul Polman more freedom to make the longer term a priority, including environmental and social sustainability. Mr. Polman said in 2012: "We're not going into the three-month rat-races. We're not working for our shareholders. We're working for the consumer, we are focused, and the shareholder gets rewarded."[12] This is a refreshing perspective, inverted from the traditional shareholder focus view. Unilever's outputs are consumer focused, and shareholder rewards are among the outcomes of that focus. Fifty percent of Unilever's growth in 2014 came from its brands that promote the company's ethical agenda, including Ben & Jerry's, Dove, and Comfort. These brands grew twice as quickly as their competitors.[13]

With every passing year, the wider business community further recognizes the importance of this longer-term horizon. In a recent interview, JPMorgan Chase CEO Jamie Dimon confidently stated: "We don't give quarterly earnings forecasts, and I don't think any CEO should. They put the company in a terrible position. You can't possibly account for all the things you need to know to create that forecast. I do believe in transparency. I'll tell people what we plan to spend on technology or how many branches we'll open. But earnings are based on decisions that have been made over the past ten years. . . . An earnings forecast suggests precision, but we can't be precise on so many factors. It gives a false sense of security."[14] In 2014, a survey of UK managers revealed that 45 percent were already realizing that their outlook at work had become longer term over the previous five years.[15] So even the vanguard leaders such as Paul Polman and Jamie Dimon are only among the first leaders to act upon what appears to be almost a ubiquitous Gen Y perspective.

Returning to our original Gen Y survey and looking at two responses together—that 43 percent want to focus on mission and only 1 percent on financial worth—indicates that more CEOs of the future will behave as Polman and Dimon have. But will the investor community tolerate this? There will be inevitable tensions, but remember that with every passing week more Gen Ys become investors, analysts, pension and asset managers themselves, and they will target companies that share their ethos. Enhancing social responsibility in word and deed and making decisions for the long haul are surely only going to increase goodwill in one's consumer base. This matters a great deal to the bottom line because, in the United States alone, there are more than ninety million Gen Ys whose aggregate net worth has exploded from $2 trillion in 2014 to $7 trillion in 2018.[16] That's a powerful stakeholder group who can choose to be either a net promoter or a net detractor for the companies they encounter.

Beyond individual examples demonstrating that companies who are focused on their purpose are rewarded by investors and customers, aggregate research has also proven that such purpose-focused firms significantly outperform their rivals. In the book *Firms of Endearment*,[17] the authors explored those organizations who are in the top 10 percent in relation to focusing on their purpose, community, customers, and employees. Their research revealed that, over the decade ending in June 2006, these firms returned 1,025 percent to their shareholders, compared to 122 percent return on investment by the S&P 500 overall. Just to be clear, this study therefore quantified that purpose-driven organizations reward their investors better than the market average by a multiple of ten!

Separate research published in *Organization Science* reached a similar conclusion. Faculty from Harvard, Pennsylvania, and Columbia Universities surveyed half a million employees across 429 firms. While these academics did not find correlation between purpose alone and financial performance, they proved that companies with strong purpose and high clarity from management exhibit stronger financial and stock market performance. The implication is that one condition of commercial success is that an organization's employees understand and believe in their collective purpose *and* have a clear path as to how that purpose will be achieved.[18]

Perhaps our ultimate question is: Are "mission" and "financial return" fundamentally in opposition to each other? Recent research indicates this is not necessarily so, and the two forces may even serve each other. A huge amount of dialogue has attempted to answer this question both in media and in conferences. The opinions are typically more definitive than one may guess and often resemble the sentiment: "The most successful companies, both in profitability and longevity, are the ones who recognize the absolute necessity of profits as well as the equally high necessity of having a purpose beyond shareholders' wealth."[19]

INSIGHTS TO ACTIONS
One Thing You Can Do Monday Morning

We know the cliché, "What gets measured gets done." Look with fresh eyes at your objectives and more specifically your Key Performance Indictors (KPIs), be they personal, team, departmental, or organizational, but ideally those within your power to recraft. Consider which ones are related to priorities that you may actually have little to no control over, such as share price, and eliminate or at least challenge those with your line manager. Take any KPI that is ultimately an outcome, and put it in a separate box under a category such as, "We'll know it was a good year when . . ." If you cannot affect those outcome KPIs on a daily basis, then extract them from your focus.

Consider the remaining KPIs. How many are customer focused? It should be most of them. If not, you may have just discovered that you're in the midst of an objective drift away from your enterprise's purpose. If you directly manage others, you should certainly also have KPIs around your people's development and engagement. Remember that Gen Ys feel a greater affiliation with the team over the company in many cases, so ensure that you have a micro-focus on how your direct reports experience work on a daily basis with their immediate colleagues and with you.

12

WORK AND LEADERSHIP FOR THE TWENTY-FIRST CENTURY

People who have been there forever, left to their own devices, are rarely in the best position to design the future. It's those who consciously listen to the constituents of the future who can understand in which direction to move.
—CRYSTAL KADAKIA[1]

We are turning the page, after more than a century, to a new chapter about how we practice capitalism in the twenty-first century. Remember how we defined generations back in chapter 2: Each generation is a reflection of its environment. Much of the friction that Gen Xs and Boomers have experienced in managing Gen Ys has been due to Ys' reaction and rebellion against the failings of business life as it has been practiced and the disadvantages of shareholder capitalism. While this stage of capitalism has produced enormous wealth, it has metastasized into a troublesome dynamic for humankind and particularly for employees. The different generations can continue to work together in parallel but incompatible paradigms or we can learn from Ys' rejection of Industrial Age management. After all, a rejection of any institution carries with it the promise of an alternative—the promise of the corporate estate that recognizes the dignity and potential of human adaptability, innovation, and empathy.

I spoke to many who despaired at the prospect of Gen Ys assuming the leadership mantles of their organizations: "They have no respect, no work ethic, no loyalty," and so on. By this point, I hope I've convinced you that this pessimism is misplaced. I've also recognized that if you study generations long enough, you see some patterns reemerge. Gen Y, and the reaction to them, reminds me of the so-called Lost Generation[2] of the 1920s, coming of age during World War I, and the expat communities that flocked to Paris to find and reinvent themselves, their professions, and how to live—creating the cultural epicenter of the Western world at that time. Unwilling to accept a culture and society that had failed them, these philosophers, writers, poets, painters, photographers, and filmmakers found themselves in Paris, not only because of its social acceptance[3] but also the exchange rate made it possible to live well in Paris on a meager income. These "lost" youths did not just tear down the conventions of the nineteenth century but built a palace in which a newborn society could rise from the ashes of war and the tourniquet of aristocratic hegemony. Poet Archibald MacLeish called the era "the greatest period of literary and artistic innovation since the Renaissance."[4] I find the analogy between the Lost Generation and Generation Y to be a fairly accurate one—in both cases, their elders lament their rejection of society's previous norms yet do not credit them for proposing valid alternatives more suited to their respective epochs.

In witnessing this rejection of the status quo, those who manage Gen Ys justifiably find the task difficult; it is not just perception. It is difficult because Yers are resisting and dismantling an entire social context sculpted in the coal fires of the Industrial Revolution. The Gen Y CEO will ultimately lead profoundly differently in many cases when he or she is finally handed the reins of his or her institution. Rather than guess or extrapolate, when I interviewed Gen Ys in researching this book, I asked them explicitly to describe how they would lead when they enter the C-suite. One might assume that, despite sharing a generational context, the Ys working in international finance versus a small creative agency, for example, would give distinctly separate answers. One of the greatest surprises of this research is the consistency of the Gen Ys' responses despite their very different backgrounds, industries, employers, or ambitions. Here's a deeper dive into the vision of the graduates of a globally recognized retail bank.

LEADERS OF THE FUTURE WILL BE . . .

The graduate trainees that I interviewed at a massive, global bank[5] were remarkably aligned as to the principles they would follow when they become senior executives or even CEOs:

- ► Career progress at their institution will be based on merit, not tenure;
- ► Gender imbalance in leadership composition and salary will finally be eliminated;
- ► They would develop more generalists, who rotate frequently through many different functions and geographies, so they are well rounded and understand the wider ecosystem, both internal and external, in which they operate. Leaders will not rise through the bank through just one function, as they often have in the past;
- ► Encourage reverse mentoring particularly between colleagues who are internally and externally facing, so senior leaders are connected to the daily life of the bank and remain connected to customers;
- ► More flexible working will not be stigmatized; assume that the ratio of contractors to full-time employees will be much higher;
- ► Colleagues will learn leadership and management skills much earlier rather than mid-career;

► Actively encourage, in word and deed, sustainability, charity and pro bono work, health and wellness;

► Cultivate and enjoy a culture that visibly demonstrates that it values its people and earns their loyalty: "My mantra will be about *people* and looking after them. 'Employees first' is true because they are the stewards of our brand and values."

I was surprised and optimistic about this remarkable vision of leadership and hopeful for society if the Gen Ys even in our financial institutions, long derided (sometimes fairly, sometimes not) for vacuuming up our collective wealth rather than redistributing it through sustainable financial services, will progress even several steps in this benign direction.

By the time you read this, Gen Y accounts for at least half of our total workforce, and in some cases, such as China, India, and sub-Saharan Africa (with more than 70 percent of the region's population below age thirty[6]), much more. As their paradigms craft the dominant lens through which we view work, management, and leadership, the shifts in our future are reasonably clear:

Practice	Yesterday and Today	Tomorrow
Where work happens.	In the office.	Anywhere, anytime.
When leaders are developed.	After they assume line management responsibilities.	Right away; leadership skills are critical for everyone.
How leaders are developed.	On courses and through coaching.	On the job, in projects, mentoring, shadowing, secondments, online . . . and through courses as needed.
When feedback occurs.	Annually or semi-annually in formal sessions.	Regularly, frequently, and informally, after any meaningful interaction or output.

Practice	Yesterday and Today	Tomorrow
How communication happens between managers and their direct reports.	Face-to-face at scheduled, formal meetings and via email.	On social media, in pick-up meetings, informally, and in social and semi-social settings.
What intelligence we value.	Intellectual intelligence.	Emotional and social intelligence (intellect is just "table stakes").
What matters to employees.	Salary and pension (golden handcuffs); ideally, friendly colleagues too.	Development opportunities, culture, and work-life balance.
How to retain employees.	Give them a raise or promotion every two to five years.	Provide constant growth and variety.
People are promoted and given development because of . . .	Tenure at the company and sometimes age.	Merit, regardless of age or time in the company.
Development happens . . .	Individually for high potentials.	In and throughout a team—a shared experience.
Former employees are . . .	Shunned and ignored. They are now the competition.	Embraced and included. They are now a potential customer or client, certainly a brand ambassador, and will hopefully return as a colleague one day.
How culture is created.	Through a process with consultants, where the best-sounding values are articulated and shared in the annual report.	Through a process with customers and employees, considering how an organization is valued by those who interact with it.

(continues)

Practice	Yesterday and Today	Tomorrow
Work is focused on . . .	Outcomes, e.g., profit.	Outputs, e.g., customer feedback and quality.
The purpose of a leader.	Maximize shareholder return.	Fulfill organizational and personal purpose, serve customers and employees, help make people great.

As our Generation Y moves into the executive offices in our organizations, be they in the private or public sector, I'm ultimately very optimistic about the future of work, management, and leadership. That Generation Y values purpose, development, personal reinvention, and work-life balance more than previous generations means that work itself should evolve in more positive directions.

The failure of our corporate philosophy of the last century is short-termism and shareholder versus stakeholder orientation. Generation Y is already reacting against this, and when they assume leadership of our companies, they may usher in a new golden age of the corporate sector working toward the better interests of their customers, employees, and society.

Today, our companies are less innovative, agile, and inspirational than their individual employees. In other words, corporate life is less human than it could be. Generation Y is telling us how to reconnect with the humanity in the communities in which we spend the majority of our lives—our companies.

The friction we currently experience because we lack understanding of Generation Y can be turned into a profound positive. We can embrace this new paradigm of work that suggests how we can lead and be led in a manner that ennobles our human spirit. To say that we must either "work to live" or "live to work" is a false dichotomy. Rather than being forced to find our tolerable trade-off point between "work to live" or "live to work," we can make work-life itself worthwhile. Surely that is a life worth working for.

INSIGHTS TO ACTIONS
One Thing You Can Do Monday Morning

I'm going to cheat with this final suggestion and urge you *just to do something*. I hope I've started a dialogue not just between you and me, but among you and your colleagues at work, wheresoever they may be. The rushing tides of Generation Y's approach to work, management, and leadership are crashing over the dykes of twentieth-century paradigms. There's really no time to delay in being part of the solution.

To start the conversation with your own team, consider convening them on Monday morning, and summarize one theme from the book that you thought was particularly relevant, timely, impactful, or important. Facilitate a brainstorming session on what you all can do to alleviate the threat or seize the opportunity. After you've listed the ideas, cross off those that are not within the team's power to implement. There's nothing more frustrating and ineffective than an action-oriented brainstorm concluding that "they," not "we," have to do something.

This tip implies that the scope of your ambition may be more limited, but that's fine. Many great movements began with small changes. In fact, it's often easier to start your movement as a bottom-up, organic tide swell. Start within your own backyard, have one-on-one conversations, talk to some customers about these issues, involve your Gen Y colleagues for sure, and use social media to sense-check your assumptions and assess the wider ecosystem. Executives have less choice to deny an initiative if they discover that the majority are clamoring for it, rather than (as they may like to imagine) one or two "well-meaning but ill-advised malcontents."

If you believe that your company is in need of change to be fit for next generation leadership, then take action now. Take heart that as the tipping point approaches when business life will more resemble "that" generation than "your" generation, you need to have already prepared your environment.

I am writing this paragraph on New Year's Eve, and I'm usually bemused by the whole charade. After all, midnight appears every other evening of the year as well. But at the same time, and only on New Year's Eve, I have to admit to myself that when the next year draws eagerly close to the present one, there is a magic frisson in dwelling on the notion that there is no better time to dispel what is no longer material from the past and sculpt a different tomorrow. Make this your New Year's Eve moment. Happy New Year.

GENERATION Z

Anxiety is the plague of the Net Generation,
kind of like smallpox, but more panicked and less itchy.
—NADIA GIOSIA[1]

We cannot have traipsed through the challenges and opportunities inherent in a Generation Y world without asking ourselves what type of world Generation Z will shape and eventually lead. Generation theory suggests that every generation reacts, at least to some extent, against some of the paradigms of their parents. If we accept that contention, then we must conclude that any given generation will more closely resemble some of the values and perspectives of their grandparents. After all, if any view (of politics, institutions, personal finances, etc.) runs along a spectrum, then to push against one side of the spectrum is to nudge toward the other side. If this is the case, then we may have to look at Gen Z's grandparents, the Baby Boomers, to forecast what some of our future may hold. This is not to say that Gen Z is just a trip back to the past, a never-ending cycle, because the

Zs' context is not identical to that of the Boomers when they were growing up. But some of Zs' values will be closer to those of their grandparents.

Unlike the "spend now, pay later," live-for-today Gen Y philosophy, Gen Zs have already shown that they may be better savers and more averse to taking on debt.[2] Consistent with these early indications, Gen Z is less interested in the state of "owning," which shackles one to financial obligations. Banks take note— home ownership may no longer be a critical component of the American dream, or indeed a symbol of having "made it" in any region.

Our Gen Zs are less addicted to technology, more likely to read a book (yes, an honest to God book). Not taken by surprise by the questions that the web has created in relation to privacy, Zs will be more cautious about how and when they share information. Raised with an acute awareness of the human impact on the environment, Gen Z may be the finest conservationist generation since that of Teddy Roosevelt. They are more accepting of the limits of resources, considering how much energy, water, fuel they use, and considerate of the trade-offs between consuming and wasting. It appears that those companies who offer services that facilitate the sharing economy, therefore, have a very bright future. From all the characteristics above, our world of work with Gen Z may be a more responsible and considerate one, with a fair degree of anxiety in relation to privacy, sustainability, and community. We may hopefully reach a more stable equilibrium between employer and employee, with both parties recognizing a twenty-first-century approach to living and working that transcends, rather than simply rejects, the Industrial Age.

ACKNOWLEDGMENTS

My sincere and eternal thanks to:

Everyone who contributed to this book via interviews and surveys. I appreciate your time, wisdom, and transparency.

The entire Duke CE Europe team for your eternal patience, enthusiasm, dedication, warmth, and professionalism, and special thanks to Jeremy Kourdi, Beth Ahlering, Sam Manning, Wendy Feher, Jonathan Besser, Deborah Zwilling-Ikpoh, John Davis, Irene Lau, Fatoumata Diallo, and Will Chu.

"My" London Business School Executive Education Management Team: Sabine Vinck, Sam Copp, Helen Kerkentzes, Paul Smith, and David Brown.

My thought leaders: Rob Goffee, Gareth Jones, Gary Hamel, Richard Hytner, Costas Markides, and Dan Cable.

Leigh Bardugo for helping me navigate this world and for always being my friend.

Ellen Kadin, Tim Burgard, and Michael Gelb for first seeing the potential of this work, and double thank you to Michael for his mentorship and the genius Foreword.

My lovely and fabulous agent, JL Stermer, and the branding

team of Hilary Pecheone and Cassandra Baim at New Leaf Literary.

JL and Joe Volpe of New Leaf, Deirdre Smerillo of Smerillo Associates, and Ronald Stroop at HarperCollins for getting the contractual arrangements squared away.

The entire enthusiastic, welcoming, professional, and supportive team at HarperCollins Leadership: my editors, Sara Kendrick and Amanda Bauch, for collaborating on this journey, and the elite marketing team of Hiram Centeno, Sicily Axton, and Sara Hardin.

Mani Sandoval and Crystal Wells of Sandoval Design.

Jeff Farr, Aubrey Khan, and Beth Metrick of Neuwirth & Associates.

Belinda Bass for the cover design.

Diana Stoney and everyone at Speaking Office and my speaker bureaus, particularly Speakers Corner, Leading Authorities International, and Gordon Poole Agency.

The patient, inspirational, and dedicated faculty of the Bellarmine English Department who taught me how to write: Patti Page, Bill Healy, Jim Harville, Chris Lorenc, and Tom Alessandri.

My mom and dad and entire family for, well, everything. Love you and thank you.

My wife and first editor, Beth. All I am is possible because of you. "It's so much more friendly with two."

ENDNOTES

Section 1

1. Douglas Broom, "Finland is the world's happiest country—again," *World Economic Forum*, March 21, 2019, https://www.weforum.org /agenda/2019/03/finland-is-the-world-s-happiest-country-again/.
2. Rob Goffee and Gareth Jones, *Why Should Anyone Work Here?* (Boston: Harvard Business Review Press, 2015), 7.

Chapter 1

1. Christopher Alexander, *A Pattern Language: Towns, Buildings, Construction* (Oxford: Oxford University Press, 1977), X.
2. Neil Howe, "The Silent Generation, 'The Lucky Few,'" *Forbes*, August 13, 2014, https://www.forbes.com/sites/neilhowe/2014/08/13 /the-silent-generation-the-lucky-few-part-3-of-7/#1590f6052c63.
3. Amy Adkins, "Millennials: The Job-Hopping Generation," *Gallup Workplace*, https://www.gallup.com/workplace/231587/millennials -job-hopping-generation.aspx.
4. Adam Kingl surveyed and interviewed ten cohorts of the Emerging Leaders Programme at London Business School from 2009 to 2014. Survey participants came from Angola, Austria, Bahrain, Belgium, Brazil, Bulgaria, Canada, China, Croatia, Egypt, France, Germany, Ghana, Greece, Hungary, India, Iran, Israel, Italy, Japan, Kazakhstan, Kuwait, Lebanon, Luxembourg, Netherlands,

Nigeria, Oman, Pakistan, Portugal, Qatar, Russian Federation, Saudi Arabia, Slovenia, South Africa, South Korea, Spain, Switzerland, Thailand, Turkey, Ukraine, United Arab Emirates, United Kingdom, United States, and Vietnam.

5. Gallup Workplace, "Item 10: I Have a Best Friend at Work," May 26, 1999, https://www.gallup.com/workplace/237530/item-best -friend-work.aspx.

6. Deloitte, "2018 Deloitte Millennial Survey: Millennials disappointed in business, unprepared for Industry 4.0," 2018, https:// www2.deloitte.com/content/dam/Deloitte/global/Documents /About-Deloitte/gx-2018-millennial-survey-report.pdf.

7. Karyn Twaronite, "Global generations: A global study on work-life challenges across generations," *EY Survey Report* (2015):1, https: //www.ey.com/Publication/vwLUAssets/Global_generations _study/$FILE/EY-global-generations-a-global-study-on-work-life-challenges-across-generations.pdf.

Chapter 2

1. Pete Townshend, 1966, https://www.azlyrics.com/lyrics/who/my generation.html.

2. Karl Mannheim, "The Problem of Generations," *Essays on the Sociology of Knowledge* (London: Routledge, 2014, first published in 1952).

3. Mannheim, *Essays on the Sociology of Knowledge.*

4. Neil Howe and William Strauss, *Generations* (New York City: William Morrow, 1992).

5. Shailesh Menon, "How tech-enabled agriculture ventures are offering farm related services via mobile phones," *Economic Times,* August 29, 2017, https://economictimes.indiatimes.com /news/economy/agriculture/how-tech-enabled-agriculture -ventures-are-offering-farm-related-services-via-mobile-phones /articleshow/60265335.cms.

6. Libby Kane, "Meet Generation Z, the 'millennials on steroids' who could lead the charge for change in the US," *Business Insider,* December 4, 2017, https://www.businessinsider.com/generation -z-profile-2017-9?r=US&IR=T.

7. Tom Brokaw, *The Greatest Generation* (New York City: Random House, 2005).

8. Rich Cohen, "The Bestest Generation," *Vanity Fair,* September 2017.

9. Douglas Copeland, *Generation X: Tales for an Accelerated Culture* (London: Abacus, 1996).

10. Samantha Raphelson, "From GIs to Gen Z (Or Is It iGen?): How Generations Get Nicknames," NPR, October 6, 2016, https://

www.npr.org/2014/10/06/349316543/don-t-label-me-origins-of
-generational-names-and-why-we-use-them?t=1558884078389.

11. Cohen, *Vanity Fair.*

12. Churches around the world reported declining numbers of parish-
ioners during Gen Xs' childhood, a trend that has yet to reverse.

13. Warren Bennis and Robert Thomas, "Crucibles of Leadership,"
Harvard Business Review, September 2002, https://hbr.org
/2002/09/crucibles-of-leadership.

14. Ryan Jenkins, "How to Design Employee Experiences That Win
Millennial Loyalty," September 12, 2017, https://www.inc.com
/ryan-jenkins/how-to-design-employee-experiences-that-win-millen
.html.

15. 2017 ELEQT survey of 1,592 respondents, of which 43 percent
were Generation Y.

16. Lynda Gratton and Andrew Scott, *The 100-Year Life* (London:
Bloomsbury, 2016).

17. Dr. Hamilton Moses, David Matheson, and Dr. E. Ray Dorsey, "The
Anatomy of Health Care in the United States," *JAMA: Journal of the
American Medical Association* (November 13, 2013).

18. "Life expectancy at birth and at age 65: OECD countries, selected
years 1980–2013," U.S. Dept. of Health and Human Services, U.S.
Government Printing Office, 2015.

19. Roger Lowenstein, "The End of Pensions," *New York Times Magazine*, October 30, 2005.

20. Jonathan Gardner, Brendan McFarland, and Ignacio Scassio, "A
tale of two countries: Defined contribution plans in the U.K. and
U.S.," Willis Towers Watson, February 24, 2017.

21. Lindsay Cook, "Can you afford to live to 100?" *Financial Times,* July
28, 2017.

22. Jen Wieczner, "Most Millennials Think They'll Be Worse Off Than
Their Parents," *Fortune*, March 1, 2016, http://fortune.com/2016
/03/01/millennials-worse-parents-retirement/.

23. This is better known in the United States as the 401(k) plan.

24. "UK wage growth slows as higher inflation starts to bite," BBC News,
April 12, 2017, https://www.bbc.co.uk/news/business-39576856.

25. "Millennials wish they had grown up in their parents' era, says a
think-tank," Sky News, September 9, 2017, https://news.sky.com
/story/millennials-wish-they-had-grown-up-in-their-parents-era-says
-a-think-tank-11026389.

26. Kate Rogers, "Adjusted for inflation, the federal minimum wage is
worth less than 50 years ago," CNBC, July 21, 2016, https://www.cnbc
.com/2016/07/21/adjusted-for-inflation-the-federal-minimum
-wage-is-worth-less-than-50-years-ago.html.

27. Laura Shin, "The Retirement Crisis: Why 68% of Americans Aren't
Saving In an Employer-Sponsored Plan," *Forbes*, April 9, 2015.

28. Kate Beioley and Josephine Cumbo, "Millennials and the gig economy left behind by pension reforms," *Financial Times*, December 18, 2017.

29. UserExperiencesWorks, "A Magazine Is an iPad That Does Not Work," YouTube, https://www.youtube.com/watch?v=aXV-yaFmQNk.

30. Kelsey Bernius, "How to Capitalize on Gen Z Email Behavior," SendGrid, December 7, 2017, https://sendgrid.com/blog/how-to -capitalize-on-genz-email-behavior/.

31. Libby Kane, "Meet Generation Z, the 'Millennials on steroids' who could lead the charge for change in the US," *Business Insider*, December 4, 2017.

Chapter 3

1. Jamie Miller, Jacob Manson, Chris Crowhurst, Paloma Faith, and Max Wolfgang, 2018, https://www.azlyrics.com/lyrics/paloma-faith/loyal.html.

2. Deloitte, "2018 Deloitte Millennial Survey: Millennials disappointed in business, unprepared for Industry 4.0," 2018.

3. Lynda Gratton and Andrew Scott, *The 100-Year Life* (London: Bloomsbury, 2016).

4. Jeremy Neuner, "40% of America's workforce will be freelancers by 2020," *Quartz*, March 20, 2013, https://qz.com/65279/40-of -americas-workforce-will-be-freelancers-by-2020/.

5. Jules Goddard, "Let's Kill Leadership," *London Business School Review*, 29, no. 1 (2018): 51.

6. Goddard, *London Business School Review*, 53.

7. Tim Titus interviewed by Adam Kingl, 2018.

8. Miguel Helft, "For Buyers of Web Start-Ups, Quest to Corral Young Talent," *New York Times*, May 17, 2011, https://www .cnbc.com/id/43075580.

9. Geoffrey Moore, *Dealing with Darwin: How Great Companies Innovate at Every Phase of Their Evolution* (Mankato: Capstone, 2006), http:// strategictoolkits.com/strategic-concepts/core-and-context/.

10. Twenty Eighty Strategic Execution and PwC 4th Annual Global Portfolio and Program Management Survey.

11. Stephanie Dube Dwilson, "The Goldman Sachs Job Interview Process," *The Nest*, https://woman.thenest.com/goldman-sachs-job -interview-process-16363.html.

12. Kristin Dudley, interviewed by Adam Kingl, 2018.

13. Mark Graban, "Henry Ford & Hospitals, Nearly 100 Years Ago," *Lean Blog*, March 25, 2014, https://www.leanblog.org/2014/03 /henry-ford-hospitals-nearly-100-years-ago/.

14. Sally Spinks, interviewed by Adam Kingl, 2018.

Chapter 4

1. Amit Chowdhry, "Lessons Learned from 4 Steve Jobs Quotes," *Forbes*, October 5, 2013, https://www.forbes.com/sites/amit chowdhry/2013/10/05/lessons-learned-from-4-steve-jobs-quotes /#5aca5bab4f69.

2. "Banks? No, thanks!" *The Economist*, October 11, 2014, https:// www.economist.com/business/2014/10/11/banks-no-thanks.

3. Richard Jolly, "Are you suffering from hurry sickness?," *Change-board*, June 27, 2018, https://www.changeboard.com/article-details /15361/are-you-suffering-from-hurry-sickness-/.

4. Jacopo Prisco, "Illusion of control: Why the world is full of buttons that don't work," *CNN Style*, September 3, 2018, https://edition .cnn.com/style/article/placebo-buttons-design/index.html.

5. Tim Elmore, "Nomophobia: A Rising Trend in Students," *Psychol-ogy Today*, September 18, 2014, https://www.psychologytoday .com/gb/blog/artificial-maturity/201409/nomophobia-rising -trend-in-students.

6. Elmore, *Psychology Today*.

7. Costas Markides, "Generation Tech: The Impact on Global Busi-ness," Global Leadership Summit presentation, 2014.

8. Daniel Bulygin, "Most Brits Can't Imagine Life Without Their Mobile—UK Tablet & Smartphone Usage," *Trendblog.net*, Novem-ber 24, 2012, https://trendblog.net/most-brits-cant-imagine-life -without-mobile/.

9. Charles Handy, *The Age of Unreason: New Thinking for a New World* (New York City: Random House Business, 1995).

10. Taking into account annual leave, national holidays, office clo-sures, and weekends.

11. Thanks to Professor Rob Goffee of London Business School for the wonderful elaboration of Handy's numbers . . . and for the joke about France.

12. Karsten Strauss, "The Growing Army of Americans Who Work from Home," *Forbes*, June 22, 2017, https://www.forbes/sites /karstenstrauss/2017/06/22/the-growing-army-of-americans-who -work-from-home/#2f92f2414ff7.

13. Laura Vanderkam, "Will Half of People Be Working Remotely by 2020?" *Fast Company*, August 14, 2014.

14. Sue Gannon, interviewed by Adam Kingl in France, March 2018.

15. Sarah Langley, interviewed by Adam Kingl in France, March 2018.

16. Stephen Parker, interviewed by Adam Kingl in London, UK, Feb-ruary 2018.

17. Goffee and Jones, *Why Should Anyone Work Here?* (Boston: Harvard Business Review Press, 2015), 131–32.

18. From the American Psychological Association's 2017 Job Skills Training and Career Development Survey, *Harvard Business Review*, March–April 2018.

19. Ethan Baron, "At Harvard, Wharton, Columbia, MBA Start-Up Fever Takes Hold," *Fortune*, January 3, 2015, http://fortune.com /2015/01/03/business-school-startups-entrepreneurs/.

20. Eight is considered to be a lucky number in Chinese and other Asian cultures.

21. Rob Goffee and Gareth Jones, *Clever: Leading Your Smartest, Most Creative People* (Boston: Harvard Business Review Press, 2009), 31.

22. From Rob Goffee in a lecture.

23. Rob Goffee and Gareth Jones, *The Character of a Corporation: How Your Company's Culture Can Make or Break Your Business* (London: Profile Books, 2003), 192.

24. Aristotle, Lesley Brown, ed., *The Nicomachean Ethics*, trans. David Ross (Oxford: Oxford World's Classics, 2009).

25. Jenny Lawson, *Furiously Happy* (London: Picador, 2016).

26. Neil Gaiman and Chris Riddell, *Art Matters: Because Your Imagination Can Change the World* (London: Headline, 2018).

27. Stephen Parker, interviewed by Adam Kingl in London, UK, February 2018.

28. Stephen Parker, interview.

Chapter 5

1. Vincelombardi.com, http://www.vincelombardi.com/quotes.html.

2. Adam Kingl surveying and interviewing ten cohorts of the Emerging Leaders Programme at London Business School from 2009 to 2014.

3. Ian Hardie, interviewed by Adam Kingl, 2018.

4. Charles O'Reilly III and Michael Tushman, "The Ambidextrous Organization," *Harvard Business Review*, April 2004.

Section 2

1. Brian Beck, "Amazon is the new Google for Product Search," *Digital Doughnut*, November 21, 2017, https://www.digitaldoughnut .com/articles/2017/november/amazon-is-the-new-google-for -product-search.

Chapter 6

1. Austin Kleon, "Beautiful things grow out of shit," Austinkleon .com, June 19, 2018, https://austinkleon.com/tag/henry-david -thoreau/page/2/.
2. I never really commonly heard the term "Silicon Valley" when I was growing up there. The area was just "the 'burbs"!
3. David Shimer, "Yale's Most Popular Class Ever: Happiness," *New York Times*, January 26, 2018.
4. Shimer, *New York Times*.
5. Shimer, *New York Times*.
6. Dan Cable, "How to activate your best self and what happens when you do," *London Business School Review*, June 26, 2016, https://www .london.edu/faculty-and-research/lbsr/how-to-activate-your-best -self-and-what-happens-when-you-do.

Chapter 7

1. Kristi Hedges, "Five Things Every Virtual Manager Should Do," *Forbes*, April 17, 2013, https://www.forbes.com/sites/work-in -progress/2013/04/17/five-things-every-virtual-manager-should -do/#183c0f716ce0.
2. I'm grateful to Moti Shahani for his collaboration with this exercise.
3. William Langewiesche, "The Human Factor," *Vanity Fair*, October 2014.
4. Katherine Phillips, Katie Liljenquist, and Margaret Neale, "Is the Pain Worth the Gain? The Advantages and Liabilities of Agreeing with Socially Distinct Newcomers," *Personality and Social Psychology Bulletin*, December 29, 2008.
5. Moti Shahani in discussion with Adam Kingl, 2009–2010, 2019.
6. Gary Hamel and Bill Breen, *The Future of Management* (Boston: Harvard Business Review Press, 2007), 229–236.
7. Hamel and Breen, *The Future of Management*.
8. Axel Franzen and Sonja Pointner, "Calling social capital: An analysis of the determinants of success on the TV quiz show 'Who Wants to Be a Millionaire?'," *Social Networks*, January 2011.
9. The 50:50 lifeline has an error probability of 15.7 percent.
10. Federico Perea and Justo Puerto, "A Simple Analysis of the TV Game 'Who Wants to Be A Millionaire?'," *Management Mathematics for European Schools* 94342, no. 1 (2001): c21.

Chapter 8

1. W.S. Gilbert, "I Am the Very Model of a Modern Major-General," Gilbert and Sullivan Archive, https://www.gsarchive.net/pirates /web_op/pirates13.html. A "'gee" is nineteenth century slang for a horse.
2. Lynda Gratton and Andrew Scott, *The 100-Year Life* (London: Bloomsbury, 2016).
3. David Rook, "The Changing Definition of Work-Life Balance," *JP Griffin Group*, August 29, 2017, https://www.griffinbenefits.com /employeebenefitsblog/the_changing_definition_of_work_life _balance.
4. Rachel Dresdale, "9 Millennials Share What Work-Life Balance Means to Them," *Forbes*, February 27, 2017, https://www.forbes .com/sites/rachelritlop/2017/02/27/9-successful-millennials -share-what-work-life-balance-means-to-them/#70940f7d7ca4.
5. Andrew Brodsky and Teresa Amabile, "The Downside of Downtime: The Prevalence and Work Pacing Consequences of Idle Time at Work," in the *Journal of Applied Psychology*, as summarized in *Harvard Business Review,* May–June 2018.
6. Jennifer Petriglieri, "Talent Management and the Dual-Career Couple," *Harvard Business Review*, May–June 2018.
7. Petriglieri, "Talent Management and the Dual-Career Couple."
8. Gary Hamel, "Bureaucracy Must Die," *Harvard Business Review*, November 4, 2014.
9. Petriglieri, "Talent Management and the Dual-Career Couple."
10. Ian McNeil, Deputy Global Head of Risk Engineering at Zurich, interviewed by Adam Kingl in London, UK, 2019.
11. A lovely phrase from the late Professor Warren Bennis.
12. Gianpiero Petriglieri, Susan Ashford, and Amy Wrzesniewski, "Thriving in the Gig Economy: How Successful Freelancers Manage the Uncertainty," *Harvard Business Review*, March–April 2018.
13. Petriglieri, Ashford, and Wrzesniewski, "Thriving in the Gig Economy: How Successful Freelancers Manage the Uncertainty."
14. Sandra Sucher and Shalene Gupta, "Layoffs That Don't Break Your Company," *Harvard Business Review,* May–June 2018.

Chapter 9

1. Mabel Mercer, https://www.lyrics.com/lyric/9909106/Mabel+ Mercer/Experiment.
2. Rian Johnson, screenwriter, *Star Wars: The Last Jedi*, https://www .imdb.com/title/tt2527336/fullcredits.

3. Nathan Bennett and G. James Lemoine, "What VUCA Really Means for You," *Harvard Business Review,* January–February 2014.

4. William Baumol, *The Cost Disease: Why Computers Get Cheaper and Health Care Doesn't* (New Haven: Yale University Press, 2013), 49.

5. Charles Dickens, *A Tale of Two Cities* (Ware: Wordsworth Classics, 1993). Originally published in 1859.

6. Kif Leswing, "Apple is flying a pirate flag over its headquarters— here's why," *Business Insider,* April 1, 2016, https://www.business insider.com/apple-is-flying-a-pirate-flag-over-its-headquarters-today -heres-why-2016-4?r=UK&IR=T.

7. "Teamwork—the Steve Jobs 1985 Macintosh Computer Team (2)," YouTube, 10:15, "Lancaster Lux," June 23, 2014, https://www .youtube.com/watch?v=BeGA1y3VPXo.

8. Hamel and Breen, *The Future of Management* (Boston: Harvard Business Review Press), 28–29.

9. Constantinos Markides and Paul Geroski, *Fast Second: How Companies Bypass Radical Innovation to Enter and Dominate New Markets* (London: John Wiley & Sons, 2004).

10. Gary Hamel and Michele Zanini, "The End of Bureaucracy," *Harvard Business Review,* November–December 2018.

11. Hamel and Zanini, "The End of Bureaucracy."

12. Zhang Ruimin, speech at Seventh Global Drucker Forum, Vienna, November 7, 2015.

13. Bill Fischer, Umberto Lago, and Fang Liu, "The Haier Road to Growth," *strategy + business,* April 27, 2015.

14. Chance Barnett, "Trends Show Crowdfunding to Surpass VC by 2016," *Forbes,* June 9, 2015, https://www.forbes/sites/chancebarnett /2015/06/09/trends-show-crowdfunding-to-surpass-vc-in-2016 /#5b637a144547.

15. Thank you to Gary Hamel for sharing this example in a lecture.

16. 40Billion, "Crowdfunding vs Venture Capital," February 7, 2018, http://www.40billion.com/post/65783.

17. Alan Boyle, "Gamers solve molecular puzzle that baffled scientists," NBCNews.com: Science News, September 18, 2011, https:// www.nbcnews.com/sciencemain/gamers-solve-molecular-puzzle -baffled-scientists-6C10402813.

18. David Bayles and Ted Orland, *Art and Fear: Observations on the Perils (and Rewards) of Artmaking* (Minneapolis: Image Continuum Press, 2002).

19. Nathan Furr, "How Failure Taught Edison to Repeatedly Innovate," *Forbes,* June 9, 2011, https://www.forbes/sites/nathanfurr /2011/06/09/how-failure-taught-edison-to-repeatedly-innovate /#46ac672c65e9.

20. Helen O'Hara, "The Secret of Pixar's Success," *Empire,* July 19, 2010, https://www.empireonline.com/movies/features/secret-pixars-success/.

21. Ed Catmull, *Creativity, Inc.* (London: Transworld Publishers, 2014).

22. Matthew Syed, "Viewpoint: How Creativity is Helped By Failure," BBC News, November 14, 2015, https://www.bbc.co.uk/news/magazine-34775411. I am indebted to Mr. Syed for these powerful examples of creativity through iteration in his fine article.

23. Syed, "Viewpoint: How Creativity is Helped by Failure."

24. David Eagleman, *Incognito: The Secret Lives of the Brain* (London: Canongate Canons, April 7, 2016).

25. Syed, "Viewpoint: How Creativity is Helped By Failure."

26. Adam Robinson, "Want to Boost Your Bottom Line? Encourage Your Employees to Work on Side Projects," Inc.com, March 12, 2018, https://www.inc.com/adam-robinson/google-employees-dedicate-20-percent-of-their-time-to-side-projects-heres-how-it-works.html.

27. Julian Birkinshaw, "Why the Best Ideas Can Come from Outside the Business: How Roche discovers new healthcare innovations," London Business School, May 3, 2017, https://www.london.edu/faculty-and-research/lbsr/diie-healthcare-innovations.

28. Birkinshaw, "Why the Best Ideas Can Come from Outside the Business: How Roche discovers new healthcare innovations."

Chapter 10

1. Robert Lopez and Jeff Marx, lyricists, https://www.themusicallyrics.com/a/36-avenue-q-musical-songs.html.

2. Abraham Maslow, *A Theory of Human Motivation* (Radford: Wilder Publications, 2013). Maslow's hierarchy of needs argues that, first, people seek satisfaction of their physical and security needs, then love and belonging, then self-esteem, and finally self-actualization.

3. Lori Goler, Janelle Gale, Brynn Harrington, and Adam Grant, "The 3 Things Employees Really Want: Career, Community, Cause," *Harvard Business Review,* February 20, 2018, https://hbr.org/2018/02/people-want-3-things-from-work-but-most-companies-are-built-around-only-one.

4. Goler, Gale, Harrington, and Grant, "The 3 Things Employees Really Want: Career, Community, Cause."

5. Adam Kingl surveying and interviewing ten cohorts of the Emerging Leaders Programme at London Business School from 2009 to 2014.

6. London.edu, "Most millennials will only work for purpose-driven firms," March 29, 2018, https://www.london.edu/news-and-events /news/most-millennials-will-only-work-for-purpose-driven-firms -1431.

7. Costas Markides, "Generation Tech: The Impact on Global Business," Global Leadership Summit presentation, 2014.

8. Eric Garton and Michael Mankins, "Engaging Your Employees Is Good, But Don't Stop There," *Harvard Business Review*, December 9, 2015.

9. Vineet Nayar, *Employees First, Customers Second: Turning Conventional Management Upside Down* (Boston: Harvard Business Review Press, 2010).

10. Sarah Langley, interviewed by Adam Kingl in France, March 2018.

11. With thanks, from conversations with Duke Corporate Education CEO Michael Chavez, 2018.

12. "The public" are the people who are neither employees nor customers but know of the company, such as the community and investors.

13. With thanks to Richard Hytner for his mentorship and advice.

14. Nike mission statement, https://about.nike.com/.

15. Google mission statement, https://www.google.com/search/how searchworks/mission/.

16. Amazon mission statement, https://www.amazon.jobs/en/working /working-amazon.

Chapter 11

1. Quote Investigator, https://quoteinvestigator.com/2015/07/23 /great-power/.

2. Peter Economy, "The (Millennial) Workplace of the Future Is Almost Here—These 3 Things Are About to Change Big Time," Inc .com, January 15, 2019, https://www.inc.com/peter-economy/the -millennial-workplace-of-future-is-almost-here-these-3-things-are -about-to-change-big-time.html.

3. Adam Kingl surveying and interviewing ten cohorts of the Emerging Leaders Program at London Business School from 2009 to 2014.

4. Troy Segal, "Enron Scandal: The Fall of a Wall Street Darling," Investopedia, May 29, 2019, https://www.investopedia.com/updates /enron-scandal-summary/.

5. Mark Zuckerberg, "Facebook IPO: Letter from Mark Zuckerberg," *The Telegraph*, February 1, 2012.

6. Warren Buffett, "2013 Letter to the Shareholders of Berkshire Hathaway, Inc.," February 28, 2014, http://www.berkshirehathaway .com/letters/2013ltr.pdf.

7. Graph produced on Yahoo Finance.

8. Michael Santoli, "The S&P500 has already met its average return for a full year, but don't expect it to stay there," CNBC, June 18, 2017, https://www.cnbc.com/2017/06/18/the-sp-500-has-already -met-its-average-return-for-a-full-year.html.

9. Ciara Linnane, "Biggest Dow winners and losers in 2017: Boeing soars to record levels, GE slumps," *MarketWatch*, January 3, 2018, https://www.marketwatch.com/story/biggest-dow-winners-and -losers-in-2017-boeing-soars-to-record-levels-while-ge-slumps -2017-12-29.

10. Vlatka Hlupic, "Aligning Beliefs, Strategies and Resources," Dukece .com, September 2018, http://www.dukece.com/insights/aligning -beliefs-strategies-resources/.

11. Hlupic, "Aligning Beliefs, Strategies and Resources."

12. Michael Bow, "Utopian Unilever is making waves: Boss Paul Polman is pushing an ethical agenda, but is it working?," *City A.M.*, July 24, 2015, http://www.cityam.com/220874/love-it-or-hate-it -utopian-unilever-making-waves.

13. Bow, "Utopian Unilever is making waves: Boss Paul Polman is pushing an ethical agenda, but is it working?".

14. Adi Ignatius, "Managers Don't Have All the Answers: A conversation with JPMorgan Chase CEO Jamie Dimon," *Harvard Business Review*, July–August 2018.

15. Tom May and David Pardey, "ILM Research Paper 5: Future trends in leadership and management," Institute of Leadership & Management (May 2014).

16. Cromwell Schubarth, "Wealthfront Raises Another $64M as it Pushes to Manage Gen Y Assets," *Silicon Valley Business Journal*, October 28, 2014, https://www.bizjournals.com/sanjose/news/2014 /10/28/wealthfront-raises-another-70m-as-it-pushes-to.html.

17. Rajendra Sisodia, David Wolfe, and Jagdish Sheth, *Firms of Endearment: How World Class Companies Profit from Passion and Purpose* (Upper Saddle River: Financial Times/Prentice Hall, 2007).

18. Claudine Gartenberg, Andrea Prat, and George Serafeim, "Corporate Purpose and Financial Performance," *Organization Science*, no. 1 (October 2018).

19. David Williams and Mary Scott, "It's Time to Balance Profits and Purpose," *Harvard Business Review Blog*, September 17, 2012, https://hbr.org/2012/09/its-time-to-balance-profits-an.

Chapter 12

1. *The NYU Dispatch*, "Pulled by the Future, not Pushed by the Past," May 22, 2019, https://wp.nyu.edu/dispatch/2019/05/22/pulled-by-the-future-not-pushed-by-the-past/.
2. The term "Lost Generation" is said to have been invented by Gertrude Stein who, in 1923, overheard an exasperated garage owner berating his young mechanic: "All of you young people who served in the war, you are a lost generation. You have no respect for anything." Ernest Hemingway, who asked Stein to be his unofficial editor for many of his works, quoted her using this term in his prologue to *The Sun Also Rises* in 1926.
3. Paris was a sanctuary from the racism one would see in America and the gender segregation, both in professional and social environments, that one would have experienced in Britain and other parts of Europe.
4. Philip Greene, *A Drinkable Feast: A Cocktail Companion to 1920s Paris* (New York: TarcherPerigee, 2018), xvii.
5. Interviews conducted in London, 2018. The institution requested anonymity.
6. Lydia Gordon, "Special Report: The World's Youngest Populations," Euromonitor International, February 13, 2012, https://blog.euromonitor.com/special-report-the-worlds-youngest-populations/.

Epilogue

1. Nadia Giosia, *Nadia G's Bitchin Kitchen Cookbook* (Guilford, CT: The Globe Pequot Press, 2009).
2. Tammy Erickson, "Preparing businesses for the next generation of workers," London.edu, June 10, 2016, https://www.london.edu/news-and-events/news/preparing-businesses-for-the-next-generation-of-workers.

BIBLIOGRAPHY

40Billion. "Crowdfunding vs Venture Capital." 40billion.com, February 7, 2018, http://www.40billion.com/post/65783.

Adkins, Amy. "Millennials: The Job-Hopping Generation." Gallup, https://www.gallup.com/workplace/231587/millennials-job-hopping-generation.aspx.

American Psychological Association. 2017 Job Skills Training and Career Development Survey. *Harvard Business Review*, March–April 2018.

Aristotle. Lesley Brown, ed. *The Nicomachean Ethics.* Translated by David Ross. Oxford: Oxford World's Classics, 2009.

Barnett, Chance. "Trends Show Crowdfunding to Surpass VC by 2016." *Forbes*, June 9, 2015, https://www.forbes/sites/chancebarnett/2015/06/09/trends-show-crowdfunding-to-surpass-vc-in-2016/#5b637a144547.

Baron, Ethan. "At Harvard, Wharton, Columbia, MBA Start-Up Fever Takes Hold." *Fortune,* January 3, 2015, http://fortune.com/2015/01/03/business-school-startups-entrepreneurs/.

Baumol, William. *The Cost Disease: Why Computers Get Cheaper and Health Care Doesn't.* New Haven: Yale University Press, 2013.

Bayles, David, and Ted Orland. *Art and Fear: Observations on the Perils (and Rewards) of Artmaking.* Minneapolis: Image Continuum Press, 2002.

Beck, Brian. "Amazon is the new Google for Product Search." Digital Doughnut, November 21, 2017, https://www.digitaldoughnut.com/articles/2017/november/amazon-is-the-new-google-for-product-search.

Beioley, Kate, and Josephine Cumbo. "Millennials and the gig economy left behind by pension reforms." *Financial Times*, December 18, 2017.

Bennett, Nathan, and G. James Lemoine. "What VUCA Really Means for You." *Harvard Business Review*, January–February 2014.

Bennis, Warren, and Robert Thomas. "Crucibles of Leadership." *Harvard Business Review*, September 2002.

Bernius, Kelsey. "How to Capitalize on Gen Z Email Behavior." Send-Grid, December 7, 2017, https://sendgrid.com/blog/how-to-capitalize-on-genz-email-behavior/.

Birkinshaw, Julian. "Why the Best Ideas Can Come from Outside the Business: How Roche discovers new healthcare innovations." *London Business School Review*, May 3, 2017, https://www.london.edu/faculty-and-research/lbsr/diie-healthcare-innovations.

Bow, Michael. "Utopian Unilever is making waves: Boss Paul Polman is pushing an ethical agenda, but is it working?" *City A.M.*, July 24, 2015, http://www.cityam.com/220874/love-it-or-hate-it-utopian-unilever-making-waves.

Boyle, Alan. "Gamers solve molecular puzzle that baffled scientists." NBCNews.com: Science News, September 18, 2011, https://www.nbcnews.com/sciencemain/gamers-solve-molecular-puzzle-baffled-scientists-6C10402813.

British Broadcasting Corporation. "UK wage growth slows as higher inflation starts to bite." BBC News, April 12, 2017, https://www.bbc.co.uk/news/business-39576856.

Brodsky, Andrew, and Teresa Amabile. "The Downside of Downtime: The Prevalence and Work Pacing Consequences of Idle Time at Work." Summarized in *Harvard Business Review*, May–June 2018.

Brokaw, Tom. *The Greatest Generation*. New York City: Random House, 2005.

Broom, Douglas. "Finland is the world's happiest country—again." *World Economic Forum*, March 21, 2019, https://www.weforum.org/agenda/2019/03/finland-is-the-world-s-happiest-country-again/.

Buffett, Warren. "2013 Letter to the Shareholders of Berkshire Hathaway, Inc." February 28, 2014, http://www.berkshirehathaway.com/letters/2013ltr.pdf.

Bulygin, Daniel. "Most Brits Can't Imagine Life Without Their Mobile—UK Tablet & Smartphone Usage." Trendblog.net, November 24, 2012, https://trendblog.net/most-brits-cant-imagine-life-without-mobile/.

Cable, Dan. "How to activate your best self and what happens when you do." *London Business School Review*, June 26, 2016, https://www.london.edu/faculty-and-research/lbsr/how-to-activate-your-best-self-and-what-happens-when-you-do.

Catmull, Ed. *Creativity, Inc.* London: Transworld Publishers, 2014.

Chowdhry, Amit. "Lessons Learned from 4 Steve Jobs Quotes." *Forbes*, October 5, 2013, https://www.forbes.com/sites/amitchowdhry/2013/10/05/lessons-learned-from-4-steve-jobs-quotes/#5aca5bab4f69.

Cohen, Rich. "The Bestest Generation." *Vanity Fair*, September 2017.

Cook, Lindsay. "Can you afford to live to 100?" *Financial Times*, July 28, 2017.

Copeland, Douglas. *Generation X: Tales for an Accelerated Culture*. London: Abacus, 1996.

Deloitte. "2018 Deloitte Millennial Survey: Millennials disappointed in business, unprepared for Industry 4.0." 2018, https://www2.deloitte .com/content/dam/Deloitte/global/Documents/About-Deloitte /gx-2018-millennial-survey-report.pdf.

Dickens, Charles. *A Tale of Two Cities*. Ware: Wordsworth Classics, 1993.

Dresdale, Rachel. "9 Millennials Share What Work-Life Balance Means to Them." *Forbes*, February 27, 2017, https://www.forbes.com/sites /rachelritlop/2017/02/27/9-successful-millennials-share-what-work -life-balance-means-to-them/#70940f7d7ca4.

Dwilson, Stephanie. "The Goldman Sachs Job Interview Process." The Nest, https://woman.thenest.com/goldman-sachs-job-interview -process-16363.html.

Eagleman, David. *Incognito: The Secret Lives of the Brain*. London: Canongate Canons, 2016.

Economy, Peter. "The (Millennial) Workplace of the Future is Almost Here—These 3 Things Are About to Change Big Time." Inc.com, January 15, 2019, https://www.inc.com/peter-economy/the -millennial-workplace-of-future-is-almost-here-these-3-things-are -about-to-change-big-time.html.

Elmore, Tim. "Nomophobia: A Rising Trend in Students." *Psychology Today*, September 18, 2014, https://www.psychologytoday.com/gb /blog/artificial maturity/201409/nomophobia-rising-trend-in -students.

Erickson, Tammy. "Preparing businesses for the next generation of workers." London.edu, June 10, 2016, https://www.london.edu /news-and-events/news/preparing-businesses-for-the-next-generation -of-workers.

Fischer, Bill, Umberto Lago, and Fang Liu. "The Haier Road to Growth." *strategy + business*, April 27, 2015.

Franzen, Axel, and Sonja Pointner. "Calling social capital: An analysis of the determinants of success on the TV quiz show 'Who Wants to Be a Millionaire?'." *Social Networks*, January 2011.

Furr, Nathan. "How Failure Taught Edison to Repeatedly Innovate." *Forbes*, June 9, 2011, https://www.forbes/sites/nathanfurr/2011/06 /09/how-failure-taught-edison-to-repeatedly-innovate/#46ac672 c65e9.

Gaiman, Neil. *Art Matters: Because Your Imagination Can Change the World*. Illustrated by Chris Riddell. London: Headline, 2018.

Gallup Workplace. "Item 10: I Have a Best Friend at Work." May 26, 1999, https://www.gallup.com/workplace/237530/item-best-friend -work.aspx.

Gardner, Jonathan, Brendan McFarland, and Ignacio Scassio. "A tale of two countries: Defined contribution plans in the U.K. and U.S." Willis Towers Watson, February 24, 2017, https://www.towerswatson .com/en/Insights/Newsletters/Americas/Insider/2017/02/a -tale-of-two-countries-defined-contribution-plans-in-the-uk-and-us.

Gartenberg, Claudine, Andrea Prat, and George Serafeim. "Corporate Purpose and Financial Performance." *Organization Science*, October 9, 2018.

Garton, Eric, and Michael Mankins. "Engaging Your Employees is Good, But Don't Stop There." *Harvard Business Review*, December 9, 2015.

Giosia, Nadia. *Nadia G's Bitchin Kitchen Cookbook*. Guilford, CT: The Globe Pequot Press, 2009.

Goddard, Jules. "Let's Kill Leadership." *London Business School Review* 29, no. 1 (2018): 51.

Goffee, Rob, and Gareth Jones. *The Character of a Corporation: How Your Company's Culture Can Make or Break Your Business*. London: Profile Books, 2003.

—. *Clever: Leading Your Smartest, Most Creative People*. Boston: Harvard Business Review Press, 2009.

—. *Why Should Anyone Work Here?* Boston: Harvard Business Review Press, 2015.

Goler, Lori, Janelle Gale, Brynn Harrington, and Adam Grant. "The Three Things Employees Really Want: Career, Community, Cause." HBR.org, February 20, 2018, https://hbr.org/2018/02/people -want-3-things-from-work-but-most-companies-are-built-around-only -one.

Gordon, Lydia. "Special Report: The World's Youngest Populations." Euromonitor International, February 13, 2012, https://blog.euro monitor.com/special-report-the-worlds-youngest-populations/.

Graban, Mark. "Henry Ford & Hospitals, Nearly 100 Years Ago." *Lean Blog*, March 25, 2014, https://www.leanblog.org/2014/03/henry-ford -hospitals-nearly-100-years-ago/.

Gratton, Lynda, and Andrew Scott. *The 100-Year Life*. London: Bloomsbury, 2016.

Greene, Philip. *A Drinkable Feast*. New York: TarcherPerigee, 2018.

Hamel, Gary. "Bureaucracy Must Die." *Harvard Business Review*, November 4, 2014.

Hamel, Gary, and Bill Breen. *The Future of Management*. Boston: Harvard Business Review Press, 2007.

Hamel, Gary, and Michele Zanini. "The End of Bureaucracy." *Harvard Business Review*, November–December 2018.

Handy, Charles. *The Age of Unreason: New Thinking for a New World*. New York City: Random House Business, 1995.

Hedges, Kristi. "Five Things Every Virtual Manager Should Do." *Forbes*, April 17, 2013, https://www.forbes.com/sites/work-in-progress/2013 /04/17/five-things-every-virtual-manager-should-do/#183c0f716ce0.

Helft, Miguel. "For Buyers of Web Start-Ups, Quest to Corral Young Talent." *New York Times*, May 17, 2011.

Hlupic, Vlatka. "Aligning Beliefs, Strategies and Resources." Dukece .com, September 2018, http://www.dukece.com/insights/aligning -beliefs-strategies-resources/.

Howe, Neil. "The Silent Generation, 'The Lucky Few.'" *Forbes*, August 13, 2014, https://www.forbes/sites/neilhowe/2014/08/13/the-silent -generation-the-lucky-few-part-3-of-7/#15e2b1cd2c63.

Howe, Neil, and William Strauss. *Generations*. New York City: William Morrow, 1992.

Ignatius, Adi. "Managers Don't Have All the Answers: A conversation with JPMorgan Chase CEO Jamie Dimon." *Harvard Business Review*, July–August 2018.

Jenkins, Ryan. "How to Design Employee Experiences that Win Millen-nial Loyalty." *Inc.*, September 12, 2017, https://www.inc.com/ryan -jenkins/how-to-design-employee-experiences-that-win-millen.html.

Jolly, Richard. "Are you suffering from hurry sickness?" *Changeboard*, June 27, 2018, https://www.changeboard.com/article-details/15361 /are-you-suffering-from-hurry-sickness-/.

Kane, Libby. "Meet Generation Z, the 'Millennials on steroids' who could lead the charge for change in the US." *Business Insider*, Decem-ber 4, 2017, https://www.businessinsider.com/generation-z-profile -2017-9?r=US&IR=T.

Kleon, Austin. "Beautiful things grow out of shit." Austinkleon.com, June 19, 2018, https://austinkleon.com/tag/henry-david-thoreau /page/2/.

Langewiesche, William. "The Human Factor." *Vanity Fair*, October 2014.

Lawson, Jenny. *Furiously Happy*. London: Picador, 2016.

Leswing, Kif. "Apply is flying a pirate flag over its headquarters—here's why." *Business Insider*, April 1, 2016, https://www.businessinsider.com /apple-is-flying-a-pirate-flag-over-its-headquarters-today-heres-why -2016-4?r=UK&IR=T.

Linnane, Ciara. "Biggest Dow winners and losers in 2017: Boeing soars to record levels, GE slumps." MarketWatch, January 3, 2018, https:// www.marketwatch.com/story/biggest-dow-winners-and-losers-in-2017 -boeing-soars-to-record-levels-while-ge-slumps-2017-12-29.

London.edu. "Most millennials will only work for purpose-driven firms." March 29, 2018, https://www.london.edu/news-and-events/news /most-millennials-will-only-work-for-purpose-driven-firms-1431.

Lowenstein, Roger. "The End of Pensions." *New York Times Magazine*, October 30, 2005.

Mannheim, Karl. "The Problem of Generations." In *Essays on the Sociology of Knowledge.* London: Routledge, 2014.

Markides, Constantinos. "Generation Tech: The Impact on Global Business." Global Leadership Summit presentation, 2014.

Markides, Constantinos, and Paul Geroski. *Fast Second: How Companies Bypass Radical Innovation to Enter and Dominate New Markets.* London: John Wiley & Sons, 2004.

Maslow, Abraham. *A Theory of Human Motivation.* Radford: Wilder Publications, 2013.

May, Tom, and David Pardey. "ILM Research Paper 5: Future trends in leadership and management." Institute of Leadership & Management, May 2014, https://www.institutelm.com/asset/86EFC960-4D5B-459B-891236D56FAB84B4/.

Menon, Shailesh. "How tech enabled agriculture ventures are offering farm related services via mobile phones." *The Economic Times,* August 29, 2017, https://economictimes.indiatimes.com/news/economy/agriculture/how-tech-enabled-agriculture-ventures-are-offering-farm-related-services-via-mobile-phones/articleshow/60265335.cms.

Moore, Geoffrey. *Dealing with Darwin: How Great Companies Innovate at Every Phase of Their Evolution.* Mankato: Capstone, 2006.

Moses, Hamilton, David Matheson, and E. Ray Dorsey. "The Anatomy of Health Care in the United States." *JAMA: Journal of the American Medical Association,* November 13, 2013.

Nayar, Vineet. *Employees First, Customers Second: Turning Conventional Management Upside Down.* Boston: Harvard Business Review Press, 2010.

Neuner, Jeremy. "40% of America's workforce will be freelancers by 2020." *Quartz,* March 20, 2013, https://qz.com/65279/40-of-americas-workforce-will-be-freelancers-by-2020/.

NYU Dispatch. "Pulled by the Future, not Pushed by the Past." May 22, 2019, https://wp.nyu.edu/dispatch/2019/05/22/pulled-by-the-future-not-pushed-by-the-past/.

O'Hara, Helen. "The Secret of Pixar's Success." *Empire,* July 19, 2010, https://www.empireonline.com/movies/features/secret-pixars-success/.

O'Reilly III, Charles, and Michael Tushman. "The Ambidextrous Organization." *Harvard Business Review,* April 2004.

Perea, Federico, and Justo Puerto. "A Simple Analysis of the TV Game 'Who Wants to Be A Millionaire?'." *Management Mathematics for European Schools* 94342, no. 1 (2001): c21.

Petriglieri, Gianpiero, Susan Ashford, and Amy Wrzesniewski. "Thriving in the Gig Economy: How Successful Freelancers Manage the Uncertainty." *Harvard Business Review,* March–April 2018.

Petriglieri, Jennifer. "Talent Management and the Dual-Career Couple." *Harvard Business Review,* May–June 2018.

Phillips, Katherine, Katie Liljenquist, and Margaret Neale. "Is the Pain Worth the Gain? The Advantages and Liabilities of Agreeing with Socially Distinct Newcomers." *Personality and Social Psychology Bulletin,* December 29, 2008.

Prisco, Jacopo. "Illusion of control: Why the world is full of buttons that don't work." CNN Style, September 3, 2018, https://edition.cnn.com /style/article/placebo-buttons-design/index.html.

Raphelson, Samantha. "From GIs to Gen Z (Or Is It iGen?): How Generations Get Nicknames." NPR, October 6, 2016, https://www.npr .org/2014/10/06/349316543/don-t-label-me-origins-of-generational -names-and-why-we-use-them?t=1558884078389.

Robinson, Adam. "Want to Boost Your Bottom Line? Encourage Your Employees to Work on Side Projects." Inc.com, March 12, 2018, https://www.inc.com/adam-robinson/google-employees-dedicate -20-percent-of-their-time-to-side-projects-heres-how-it-works .html.

Rogers, Kate. "Adjusted for inflation, the federal minimum wage is worth less than 50 years ago." CNBC, July 21, 2016, https://www .cnbc.com/2016/07/21/adjusted-for-inflation-the-federal-minimum -wage-is-worth-less-than-50-years-ago.html.

Rook, David. "The Changing Definition of Work-Life Balance." JP Griffin Group, August 29, 2017, https://www.griffinbenefits.com/employee benefitsblog/the_changing_definition_of_work_life_balance.

Santoli, Michael. "The S&P500 has already met its average return for a full year, but don't expect it to stay there." CNBC, June 18, 2017, https://www.cnbc.com/2017/06/18/the-sp-500-has-already-met-its -average-return-for-a-full-year.html.

Schubarth, Cromwell. "Wealthfront Raises Another $64M as it Pushes to Manage Gen Y Assets." *Silicon Valley Business Journal,* October 28, 2014, https://www.bizjournals.com/sanjose/news/2014/10/28 /wealthfront-raises-another-70m-as-it-pushes-to.html.

Segal, Troy. "Enron Scandal: The Fall of a Wall Street Darling," Investopedia, May 29, 2019, https://www.investopedia.com/updates/enron -scandal-summary/.

Shimer, David. "Yale's Most Popular Class Ever: Happiness." *New York Times,* January 26, 2018.

Shin, Laura. "The Retirement Crisis: Why 68% of Americans Aren't Saving In an Employer-Sponsored Plan." *Forbes,* April 9, 2015, https://www.forbes/sites/laurashin/2015/04/09/the-retirement -crisis-why-68-of-americans-arent-saving-in-an-employer-sponsored -plan/#67d92cc02152.

Sisodia, Rajendra, David Wolfe, and Jagdish Sheth. *Firms of Endearment: How World Class Companies Profit from Passion and Purpose.* Upper Saddle River, NJ: Financial Times/Prentice Hall, 2007.

Sky News. "Millennials wish they had grown up in their parents' era, says a think tank." September 9, 2017, https://news.sky.com/story /millennials-wish-they-had-grown-up-in-their-parents-era-says-a-think -tank-11026389.

Strauss, Karsten. "The Growing Army of Americans Who Work from Home." *Forbes*, June 22, 2017, https://www.forbes/sites/karsten strauss/2017/06/22/the-growing-army-of-americans-who-work-from -home/#2f92f2414ff7.

Sucher, Sandra, and Shalene Gupta. "Layoffs That Don't Break Your Company." *Harvard Business Review*, May–June 2018.

Syed, Matthew. "Viewpoint: How creativity is helped by failure." BBC News, November 14, 2015, https://www.bbc.co.uk/news/magazine -34775411.

Twaronite, Karyn. "Global generations, A global study on work-life challenges across generations." EY survey report, 2015, https://www.ey .com/Publication/vwLUAssets/EY-global-generations-a-global -study-on-work-life-challenges-across-generations/$FILE/EY -global-generations-a-global-study-on-work-life-challenges-across -generations.pdf.

United States Dept. of Health and Human Services. "Life expectancy at birth and at age 65: OECD countries, selected years 1980–2013." U.S. Government Printing Office, 2015.

Vanderkam, Laura. "Will Half of People Be Working Remotely by 2020?" *Fast Company*, August 14, 2014.

Wieczner, Jen. "Most Millennials Think They'll Be Worse Off Than Their Parents." *Fortune*, March 1, 2016, http://fortune.com/2016 /03/01/millennials-worse-parents-retirement/.

Williams, David, and Mary Scott. "It's Time to Balance Profits and Purpose." *Harvard Business Review Blog*, September 17, 2012, https://hbr .org/2012/09/its-time-to-balance-profits-an.

Zuckerberg, Mark. "Facebook IPO: Letter from Mark Zuckerberg." *The Telegraph*, February 1, 2012.

ABOUT THE AUTHOR

ADAM KINGL is an author, teacher, facilitator, keynote speaker, and consultant. He was previously the Regional Managing Director, Europe, for Duke Corporate Education, the customized executive education arm of the Fuqua School of Business at Duke University. Previously, Adam was the Executive Director of Thought Leadership and Learning Solutions at London Business School. Adam was also an Associate of the Management Lab and has served on the steering committee for the European Foundation for Management Development.

Adam's corporate clients have included ADNOC, Aldar Properties, Anglo American, Carlsberg, Daimler, Ericsson, Heidelberg Cement, HSBC, Nestlé, Oman Oil, Orica, Scandinavian Airlines, Suntory, and UBS. Prior to working in business schools, Adam worked for the creative agency Just Add Water in the UK and US, collaborating with clients including BP, De Beers, Disney, LVMH, Pixar, Tesco, and Zurich Insurance. He also worked in the media and entertainment industries in both business and creative functions.

Adam has contributed to and been interviewed by publications including the *Financial Times, Sunday Times,* the *Guardian, Fast*

Company, Accenture Connections with Leading Thinkers, *BizEd*, Changeboard, *European Business Review, Business Strategy Review*, Personnel Today, *London Business School Review, Dialogue, Business News Daily*, Employee Engagement Today, *City A.M., Management Today*, Employee Benefits, Dubai Eye (radio), *Gulf News*, the *National* (UAE), Alrroya (UAE), *Business Pioneer, South China Morning Post, Hong Kong Economic Times, HR Magazine* (UK, Middle East, and Hong Kong editions), *HR Grapevine*, MEED Business Intelligence, Tokyo MIX (TV), and the Institute of Leadership and Management.

He has spoken at many conferences, including the Global Leadership Summit, FT-Coca Cola Enterprises Future of Sustainability Summit, Changeboard Future Talent Conference, HR Directors Business Summit, Employee Benefits Connect, Strategic HR Network Leadership and Talent Conference, European HR Directors International Business Summit, HR Strategy Forum, the CIPD Learning & Development Conference, and the Talent Engagement Conference.

Adam earned degrees from London Business School, UCLA, and Yale. He was raised in Silicon Valley and now lives in London. Visit his website at www.adamkingl.com.

INDEX